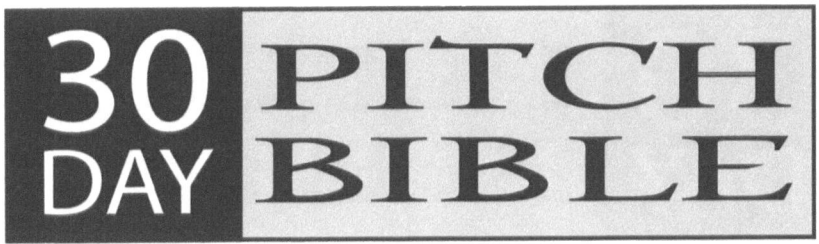

30 DAY PITCH BIBLE

The 30 day organized JUMP START to project creation.

A Kaiser Studio Production

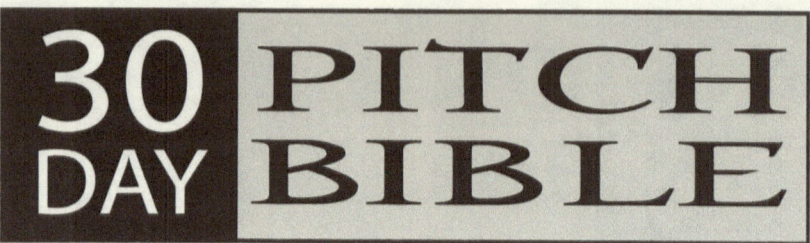

30 DAY PITCH BIBLE

The 30 day organized JUMP START to project creation.

Project Name	
Author	
Artist	
Date	

The PLANNER SECTION

In this section you are to plan out your 30 day production pipeline. Establish your monthly, weekly, and daily tasks in order to establish concrete deadlines and goals.

EUREKA

P L A N N E R

I D E A S

S T O R Y

C H A R A C T E R

E N V I R O N M E N T S

A S S E T S

S T O R Y B O A R D S

O P E N

Monthly To Do

PLANNER

IDEAS

STORY

CHARACTER

ENVIRONMENTS

ASSETS

STORY BOARDS

OPEN

Sunday	Monday	Tuesday	Wednesday	Thursday	Friday	Saturday

End Goal

EUREKA

Weekly To Do

Week One
- [ ] _____
- [ ] _____
- [ ] _____
- [ ] _____
- [ ] _____
- [ ] _____

Week Two
- [ ] _____
- [ ] _____
- [ ] _____
- [ ] _____
- [ ] _____
- [ ] _____

Week Three
- [ ] _____
- [ ] _____
- [ ] _____
- [ ] _____
- [ ] _____
- [ ] _____

Week Four
- [ ] _____
- [ ] _____
- [ ] _____
- [ ] _____
- [ ] _____
- [ ] _____

Notes

EUREKA

PLANNER

IDEAS

STORY

CHARACTER

ENVIRONMENTS

ASSETS

STORY BOARDS

OPEN

PLANNER

IDEAS

STORY

CHARACTER

ENVIRON MENTS

ASSETS

STORY BOARDS

OPEN

Daily To Do

Tasks

○
○
○
○
○
○
○
○
○
○
○
○

Website/Contacts

Notes

EUREKA

1am	
2am	
3am	
4am	
5am	
6am	
7am	
8am	
9am	
10am	
11am	
NOON	
1pm	
2pm	
3pm	
4pm	
5pm	
6pm	
7pm	
8pm	
9pm	
10pm	
11pm	
Mid-Night	

Daily To Do

1am	
2am	
3am	
4am	
5am	
6am	
7am	
8am	
9am	
10am	
11am	
NOON	
1pm	
2pm	
3pm	
4pm	
5pm	
6pm	
7pm	
8pm	
9pm	
10pm	
11pm	
Mid-Night	

Tasks

Website/Contacts

Notes

EUREKA

PLANNER

IDEAS

STORY

CHARACTER

ENVIRONMENTS

ASSETS

STORY BOARDS

OPEN

Daily To Do

IDEAS

STORY

CHARACTER

ENVIRON MENTS

ASSETS

STORY BOARDS

OPEN

Tasks

- ○
- ○
- ○
- ○
- ○
- ○
- ○
- ○
- ○
- ○
- ○
- ○

Website/Contacts

_____

_____

_____

_____

_____

Notes

EUREKA

1am	
2am	
3am	
4am	
5am	
6am	
7am	
8am	
9am	
10am	
11am	
NOON	
1pm	
2pm	
3pm	
4pm	
5pm	
6pm	
7pm	
8pm	
9pm	
10pm	
11pm	
Mid-Night	

Daily To Do

1am	
2am	
3am	
4am	
5am	
6am	
7am	
8am	
9am	
10am	
11am	
NOON	
1pm	
2pm	
3pm	
4pm	
5pm	
6pm	
7pm	
8pm	
9pm	
10pm	
11pm	
Mid-Night	

Tasks

○
○
○
○
○
○
○
○
○
○
○

Website/Contacts

Notes

EUREKA

PLANNER

IDEAS

STORY

CHARACTER

ENVIRONMENTS

ASSETS

STORY BOARDS

OPEN

Daily To Do

PLANNER

IDEAS

STORY

CHARACTER

ENVIRONMENTS

ASSETS

STORY BOARDS

OPEN

Tasks

- ○
- ○
- ○
- ○
- ○
- ○
- ○
- ○
- ○
- ○
- ○
- ○

Website/Contacts

Notes

EUREKA

1am	
2am	
3am	
4am	
5am	
6am	
7am	
8am	
9am	
10am	
11am	
NOON	
1pm	
2pm	
3pm	
4pm	
5pm	
6pm	
7pm	
8pm	
9pm	
10pm	
11pm	
Mid-Night	

Daily To Do

PLANNER

IDEAS

STORY

CHARACTER

ENVIRONMENTS

ASSETS

STORY BOARDS

OPEN

1am	
2am	
3am	
4am	
5am	
6am	
7am	
8am	
9am	
10am	
11am	
NOON	
1pm	
2pm	
3pm	
4pm	
5pm	
6pm	
7pm	
8pm	
9pm	
10pm	
11pm	
Mid-Night	

Tasks

Website/Contacts

Notes

EUREKA

Daily To Do

IDEAS

STORY

CHARACTER

ENVIRONMENTS

ASSETS

STORY BOARDS

OPEN

Tasks

- ◯
- ◯
- ◯
- ◯
- ◯
- ◯
- ◯
- ◯
- ◯
- ◯
- ◯
- ◯

Website/Contacts

Notes

EUREKA

1am	
2am	
3am	
4am	
5am	
6am	
7am	
8am	
9am	
10am	
11am	
NOON	
1pm	
2pm	
3pm	
4pm	
5pm	
6pm	
7pm	
8pm	
9pm	
10pm	
11pm	
Mid-Night	

Daily To Do

1am	
2am	
3am	
4am	
5am	
6am	
7am	
8am	
9am	
10am	
11am	
NOON	
1pm	
2pm	
3pm	
4pm	
5pm	
6pm	
7pm	
8pm	
9pm	
10pm	
11pm	
Mid-Night	

Tasks

Website/Contacts

Notes

EUREKA

PLANNER

IDEAS

STORY

CHARACTER

ENVIRONMENTS

ASSETS

STORY BOARDS

OPEN

Daily To Do

PLANNER

IDEAS

STORY

CHARACTER

ENVIRONMENTS

ASSETS

STORY BOARDS

OPEN

Tasks

Website/Contacts

Notes

EUREKA

1am	
2am	
3am	
4am	
5am	
6am	
7am	
8am	
9am	
10am	
11am	
NOON	
1pm	
2pm	
3pm	
4pm	
5pm	
6pm	
7pm	
8pm	
9pm	
10pm	
11pm	
Mid-Night	

Daily To Do

1am	
2am	
3am	
4am	
5am	
6am	
7am	
8am	
9am	
10am	
11am	
NOON	
1pm	
2pm	
3pm	
4pm	
5pm	
6pm	
7pm	
8pm	
9pm	
10pm	
11pm	
Mid-Night	

Tasks

Website/Contacts

Notes

EUREKA

PLANNER

IDEAS

STORY

CHARACTER

ENVIRONMENTS

ASSETS

STORY BOARDS

OPEN

Daily To Do

Tasks

IDEAS

STORY

CHARACTER

ENVIRON MENTS

ASSETS

STORY BOARDS

OPEN

Website/Contacts

Notes

EUREKA

1am	
2am	
3am	
4am	
5am	
6am	
7am	
8am	
9am	
10am	
11am	
NOON	
1pm	
2pm	
3pm	
4pm	
5pm	
6pm	
7pm	
8pm	
9pm	
10pm	
11pm	
Mid-Night	

Daily To Do

1am	
2am	
3am	
4am	
5am	
6am	
7am	
8am	
9am	
10am	
11am	
NOON	
1pm	
2pm	
3pm	
4pm	
5pm	
6pm	
7pm	
8pm	
9pm	
10pm	
11pm	
Mid-Night	

Tasks

- ◯
- ◯
- ◯
- ◯
- ◯
- ◯
- ◯
- ◯
- ◯
- ◯
- ◯
- ◯

Website/Contacts

Notes

EUREKA

PLANNER

IDEAS

STORY

CHARACTER

ENVIRONMENTS

ASSETS

STORY BOARDS

OPEN

PLANNER

IDEAS

STORY

CHARACTER

ENVIRONMENTS

ASSETS

STORY BOARDS

OPEN

Daily To Do

Tasks

- ◯
- ◯
- ◯
- ◯
- ◯
- ◯
- ◯
- ◯
- ◯
- ◯
- ◯
- ◯

Website/Contacts

Notes

EUREKA

1am	
2am	
3am	
4am	
5am	
6am	
7am	
8am	
9am	
10am	
11am	
NOON	
1pm	
2pm	
3pm	
4pm	
5pm	
6pm	
7pm	
8pm	
9pm	
10pm	
11pm	
Mid-Night	

Daily To Do

1am	
2am	
3am	
4am	
5am	
6am	
7am	
8am	
9am	
10am	
11am	
NOON	
1pm	
2pm	
3pm	
4pm	
5pm	
6pm	
7pm	
8pm	
9pm	
10pm	
11pm	
Mid-Night	

Tasks

Website/Contacts

Notes

EUREKA

PLANNER

IDEAS

STORY

CHARACTER

ENVIRONMENTS

ASSETS

STORY BOARDS

OPEN

PLANNER

IDEAS

STORY

CHARACTER

ENVIRONMENTS

ASSETS

STORY BOARDS

OPEN

Daily To Do

Tasks

- ⭕
- ⭕
- ⭕
- ⭕
- ⭕
- ⭕
- ⭕
- ⭕
- ⭕
- ⭕
- ⭕
- ⭕

Website/Contacts

Notes

EUREKA

1am	
2am	
3am	
4am	
5am	
6am	
7am	
8am	
9am	
10am	
11am	
NOON	
1pm	
2pm	
3pm	
4pm	
5pm	
6pm	
7pm	
8pm	
9pm	
10pm	
11pm	
Mid-Night	

Daily To Do

1am	
2am	
3am	
4am	
5am	
6am	
7am	
8am	
9am	
10am	
11am	
NOON	
1pm	
2pm	
3pm	
4pm	
5pm	
6pm	
7pm	
8pm	
9pm	
10pm	
11pm	
Mid-Night	

Tasks

Website/Contacts

Notes

EUREKA

IDEAS

STORY

CHARACTER

ENVIRONMENTS

ASSETS

STORY BOARDS

OPEN

Daily To Do

IDEAS

STORY

CHARACTER

ENVIRON MENTS

ASSETS

STORY BOARDS

OPEN

Tasks

○	
○	
○	
○	
○	
○	
○	
○	
○	
○	
○	
○	

Website/Contacts

Notes

EUREKA

1am	
2am	
3am	
4am	
5am	
6am	
7am	
8am	
9am	
10am	
11am	
NOON	
1pm	
2pm	
3pm	
4pm	
5pm	
6pm	
7pm	
8pm	
9pm	
10pm	
11pm	
Mid-Night	

Daily To Do

1am	
2am	
3am	
4am	
5am	
6am	
7am	
8am	
9am	
10am	
11am	
NOON	
1pm	
2pm	
3pm	
4pm	
5pm	
6pm	
7pm	
8pm	
9pm	
10pm	
11pm	
Mid-Night	

Tasks

- ○
- ○
- ○
- ○
- ○
- ○
- ○
- ○
- ○
- ○
- ○
- ○

Website/Contacts

Notes

EUREKA

PLANNER

IDEAS

STORY

CHARACTER

ENVIRONMENTS

ASSETS

STORY BOARDS

OPEN

Daily To Do

IDEAS

STORY

CHARACTER

ENVIRON MENTS

ASSETS

STORY BOARDS

OPEN

Tasks

○
○
○
○
○
○
○
○
○
○
○
○

Website/Contacts

Notes

EUREKA

1am	
2am	
3am	
4am	
5am	
6am	
7am	
8am	
9am	
10am	
11am	
NOON	
1pm	
2pm	
3pm	
4pm	
5pm	
6pm	
7pm	
8pm	
9pm	
10pm	
11pm	
Mid-Night	

Daily To Do

1am	
2am	
3am	
4am	
5am	
6am	
7am	
8am	
9am	
10am	
11am	
NOON	
1pm	
2pm	
3pm	
4pm	
5pm	
6pm	
7pm	
8pm	
9pm	
10pm	
11pm	
Mid-Night	

Tasks

- ○
- ○
- ○
- ○
- ○
- ○
- ○
- ○
- ○
- ○
- ○
- ○

Website/Contacts

Notes

EUREKA

PLANNER

IDEAS

STORY

CHARACTER

ENVIRONMENTS

ASSETS

STORY BOARDS

OPEN

Daily To Do

IDEAS

STORY

CHARACTER

ENVIRONMENTS

ASSETS

STORY BOARDS

OPEN

Tasks

- ◯
- ◯
- ◯
- ◯
- ◯
- ◯
- ◯
- ◯
- ◯
- ◯
- ◯
- ◯

Website/Contacts

Notes

EUREKA

1am	
2am	
3am	
4am	
5am	
6am	
7am	
8am	
9am	
10am	
11am	
NOON	
1pm	
2pm	
3pm	
4pm	
5pm	
6pm	
7pm	
8pm	
9pm	
10pm	
11pm	
Mid-Night	

Daily To Do

1am	
2am	
3am	
4am	
5am	
6am	
7am	
8am	
9am	
10am	
11am	
NOON	
1pm	
2pm	
3pm	
4pm	
5pm	
6pm	
7pm	
8pm	
9pm	
10pm	
11pm	
Mid-Night	

Tasks

Website/Contacts

Notes

EUREKA

PLANNER

IDEAS

STORY

CHARACTER

ENVIRONMENTS

ASSETS

STORY BOARDS

OPEN

Daily To Do

IDEAS

STORY

CHARACTER

ENVIRON MENTS

ASSETS

STORY BOARDS

OPEN

Tasks

- ◯
- ◯
- ◯
- ◯
- ◯
- ◯
- ◯
- ◯
- ◯
- ◯
- ◯
- ◯
- ◯

Website/Contacts

Notes

EUREKA

1am	
2am	
3am	
4am	
5am	
6am	
7am	
8am	
9am	
10am	
11am	
NOON	
1pm	
2pm	
3pm	
4pm	
5pm	
6pm	
7pm	
8pm	
9pm	
10pm	
11pm	
Mid-Night	

Daily To Do

1am	
2am	
3am	
4am	
5am	
6am	
7am	
8am	
9am	
10am	
11am	
NOON	
1pm	
2pm	
3pm	
4pm	
5pm	
6pm	
7pm	
8pm	
9pm	
10pm	
11pm	
Mid-Night	

Tasks

- ○
- ○
- ○
- ○
- ○
- ○
- ○
- ○
- ○
- ○
- ○
- ○

Website/Contacts

Notes

EUREKA

I D E A S

S T O R Y

C H A R A C T E R

E N V I R O N M E N T S

A S S E T S

S T O R Y B O A R D S

O P E N

Daily To Do

PLANNER

IDEAS

STORY

CHARACTER

ENVIRON MENTS

ASSETS

STORY BOARDS

OPEN

Tasks

- ○
- ○
- ○
- ○
- ○
- ○
- ○
- ○
- ○
- ○
- ○
- ○

Website/Contacts

Notes

EUREKA

1am	
2am	
3am	
4am	
5am	
6am	
7am	
8am	
9am	
10am	
11am	
NOON	
1pm	
2pm	
3pm	
4pm	
5pm	
6pm	
7pm	
8pm	
9pm	
10pm	
11pm	
Mid-Night	

Daily To Do

1am	
2am	
3am	
4am	
5am	
6am	
7am	
8am	
9am	
10am	
11am	
NOON	
1pm	
2pm	
3pm	
4pm	
5pm	
6pm	
7pm	
8pm	
9pm	
10pm	
11pm	
Mid-Night	

Tasks

Website/Contacts

Notes

EUREKA

PLANNER

IDEAS

STORY

CHARACTER

ENVIRONMENTS

ASSETS

STORY BOARDS

OPEN

Daily To Do

Tasks

IDEAS

STORY

CHARACTER

ENVIRONMENTS

ASSETS

STORY BOARDS

OPEN

Website/Contacts

Notes

EUREKA

1am	
2am	
3am	
4am	
5am	
6am	
7am	
8am	
9am	
10am	
11am	
NOON	
1pm	
2pm	
3pm	
4pm	
5pm	
6pm	
7pm	
8pm	
9pm	
10pm	
11pm	
Mid-Night	

Daily To Do

1am	
2am	
3am	
4am	
5am	
6am	
7am	
8am	
9am	
10am	
11am	
NOON	
1pm	
2pm	
3pm	
4pm	
5pm	
6pm	
7pm	
8pm	
9pm	
10pm	
11pm	
Mid-Night	

Tasks

Website/Contacts

Notes

EUREKA

PLANNER

IDEAS

STORY

CHARACTER

ENVIRONMENTS

ASSETS

STORYBOARDS

OPEN

Daily To Do

IDEAS

STORY

CHARACTER

ENVIRON MENTS

ASSETS

STORY BOARDS

OPEN

Tasks

○	
○	
○	
○	
○	
○	
○	
○	
○	
○	
○	
○	

Website/Contacts

Notes

EUREKA

1am	
2am	
3am	
4am	
5am	
6am	
7am	
8am	
9am	
10am	
11am	
NOON	
1pm	
2pm	
3pm	
4pm	
5pm	
6pm	
7pm	
8pm	
9pm	
10pm	
11pm	
Mid-Night	

Daily To Do

1am	
2am	
3am	
4am	
5am	
6am	
7am	
8am	
9am	
10am	
11am	
NOON	
1pm	
2pm	
3pm	
4pm	
5pm	
6pm	
7pm	
8pm	
9pm	
10pm	
11pm	
Mid-Night	

Tasks

Website/Contacts

Notes

EUREKA

IDEAS

STORY

CHARACTER

ENVIRONMENTS

ASSETS

STORY BOARDS

OPEN

PLANNER

IDEAS

STORY

CHARACTER

ENVIRONMENTS

ASSETS

STORYBOARDS

OPEN

The IDEA SECTION

In this section you should brainstorm your ideas for your project.
Let your mind run free and put everything down on paper.
The sky is the limit.

EUREKA

Reference

Notes

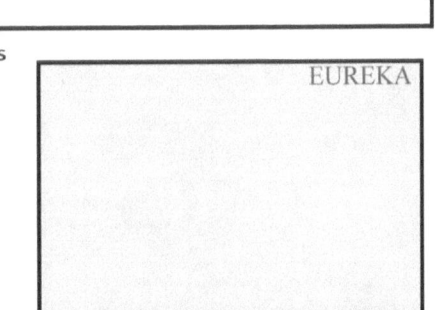

EUREKA

PLANNER

IDEAS

STORY

CHARACTER

ENVIRONMENTS

ASSETS

STORY BOARDS

OPEN

Reference

PLANNER

IDEAS

STORY

CHARACTER

ENVIRONMENTS

ASSETS

STORY BOARDS

OPEN

Reference Images/ Sketches

Notes

EUREKA

Reference

Reference Images/ Sketches

Notes

EUREKA

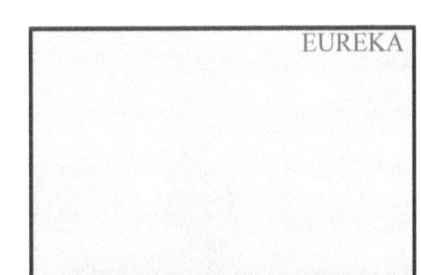

PLANNER

IDEAS

STORY

CHARACTER

ENVIRONMENTS

ASSETS

STORY BOARDS

OPEN

PLANNER

IDEAS

STORY

CHARACTER

ENVIRONMENTS

ASSETS

STORY BOARDS

OPEN

Reference

Reference Images/ Sketches

Notes

EUREKA

Reference

Notes

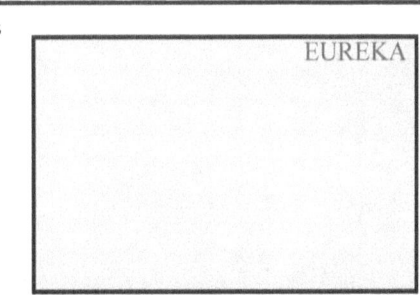

EUREKA

PLANNER

IDEAS

STORY

CHARACTER

ENVIRON MENTS

ASSETS

STORY BOARDS

OPEN

PLANNER

IDEAS

STORY

CHARACTER

ENVIRONMENTS

ASSETS

STORY BOARDS

OPEN

Reference

Reference Images/ Sketches

Notes

EUREKA

Reference

Notes

EUREKA

PLANNER

IDEAS

STORY

CHARACTER

ENVIRONMENTS

ASSETS

STORY BOARDS

OPEN

Ideas/Concepts

PLANNER

IDEAS

STORY

CHARACTER

ENVIRONMENTS

ASSETS

STORY BOARDS

OPEN

Thumbs

Thumbs

Thumbs

Thumbs

Sketches

Story

EUREKA

Ideas/Concepts

PLANNER

IDEAS

STORY

CHARACTER

ENVIRONMENTS

ASSETS

STORY BOARDS

OPEN

Thumbs   Thumbs   Thumbs   Thumbs

Story   Sketches

EUREKA

Ideas/Concepts

IDEAS

STORY

CHARACTER

ENVIRONMENTS

ASSETS

STORY BOARDS

OPEN

Thumbs

Thumbs

Thumbs

Thumbs

Sketches

Story

EUREKA

Ideas/Concepts

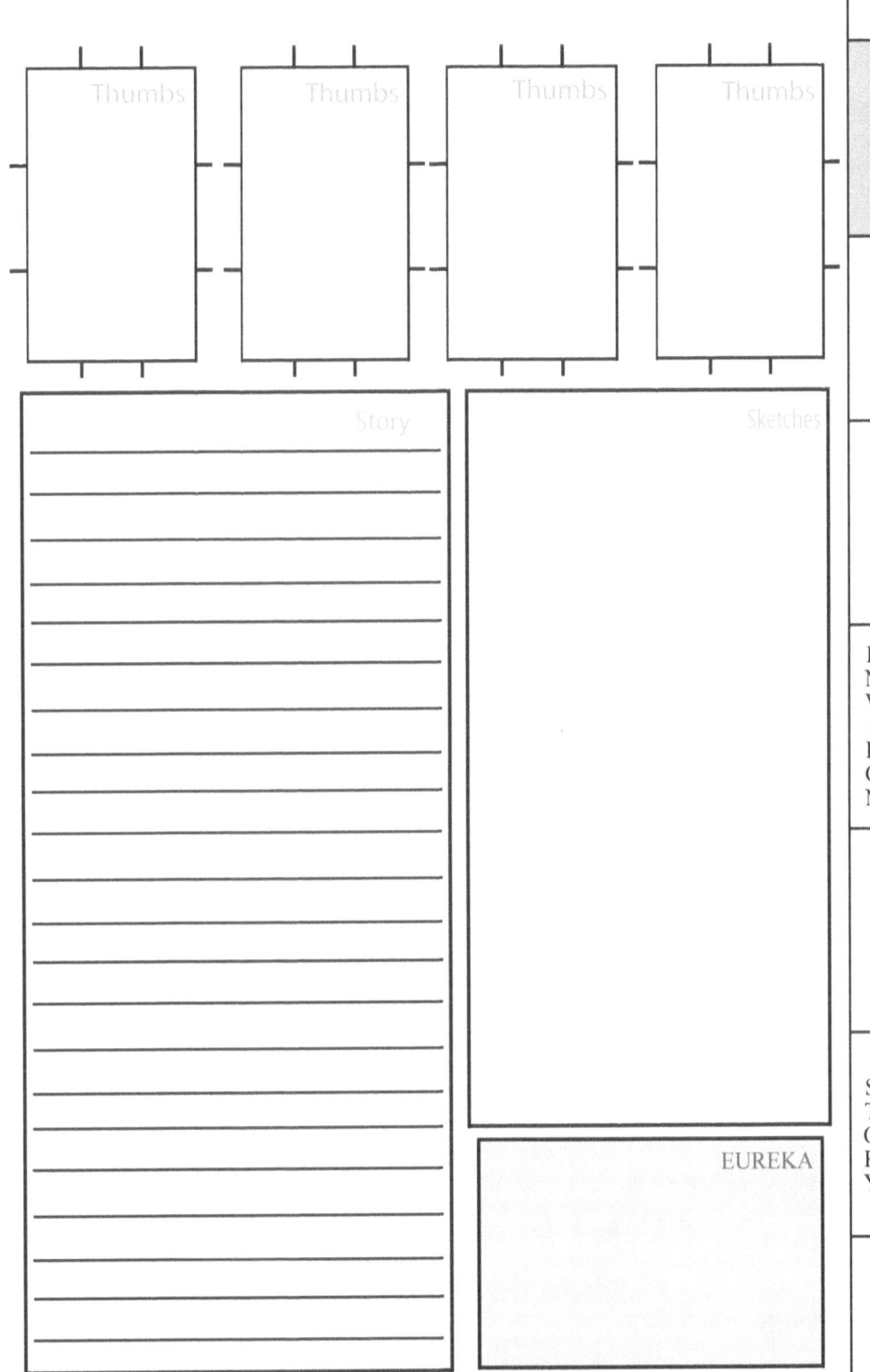

Thumbs

Thumbs

Thumbs

Thumbs

Story

Sketches

EUREKA

PLANNER

IDEAS

STORY

CHARACTER

ENVIRONMENTS

ASSETS

STORY BOARDS

OPEN

Ideas/Concepts

PLANNER

IDEAS

STORY

CHARACTER

ENVIRONMENTS

ASSETS

STORYBOARDS

OPEN

Thumbs

Thumbs

Thumbs

Thumbs

Sketches

Story

EUREKA

Ideas/Concepts

PLANNER
IDEAS
STORY
CHARACTER
ENVIRONMENTS
ASSETS
STORY BOARDS
OPEN

Thumbs   Thumbs   Thumbs   Thumbs

Story

Sketches

EUREKA

Ideas/Concepts

Thumbs

Thumbs

Thumbs

Thumbs

Sketches

Story

EUREKA

Ideas/Concepts

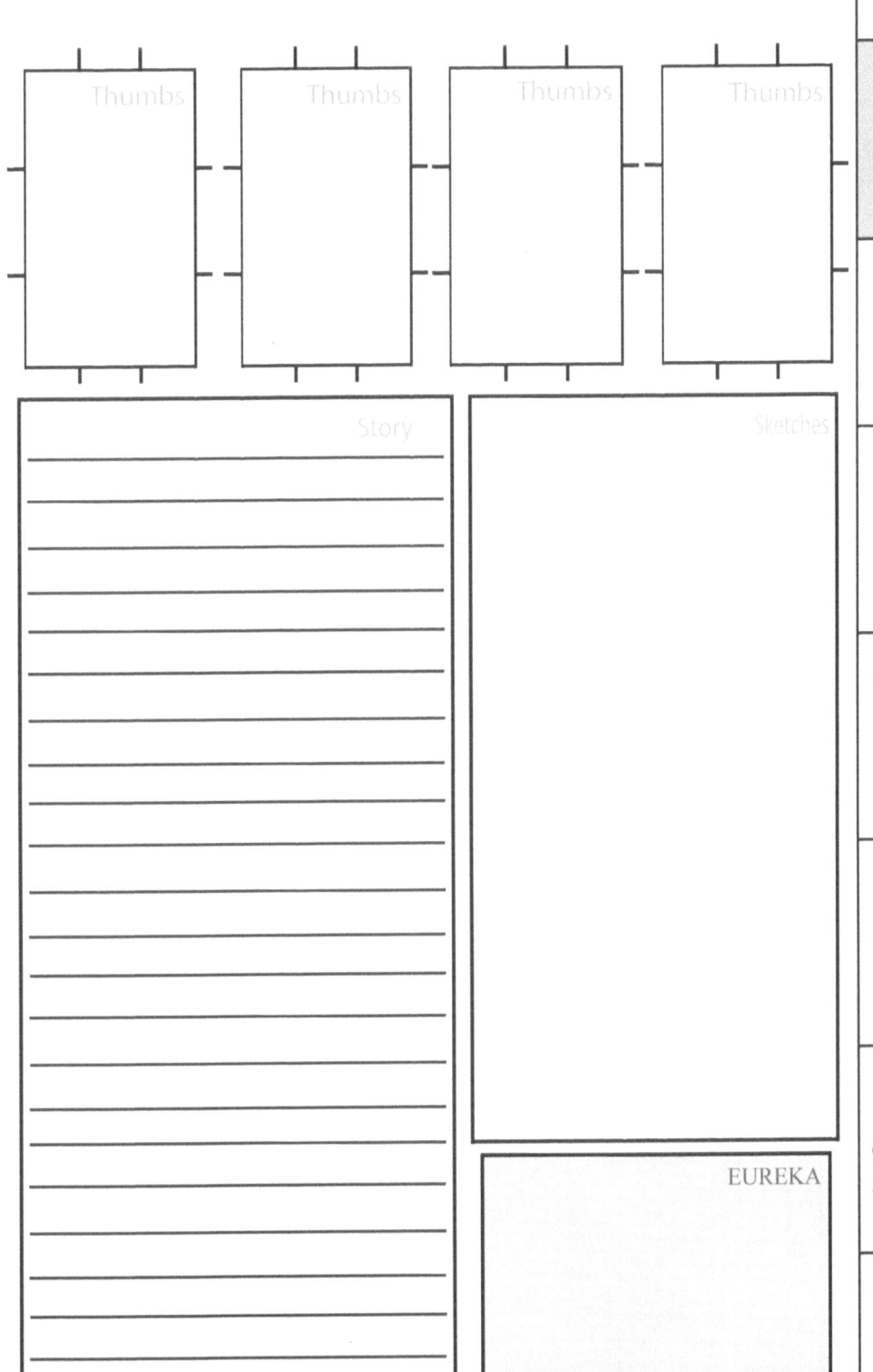

Thumbs   Thumbs   Thumbs   Thumbs

Story

Sketches

EUREKA

PLANNER

IDEAS

STORY

CHARACTER

ENVIRONMENTS

ASSETS

STORYBOARDS

OPEN

Ideas/Concepts

PLANNER

IDEAS

STORY

CHARACTER

ENVIRONMENTS

ASSETS

STORY BOARDS

OPEN

Thumbs

Thumbs

Thumbs

Thumbs

Sketches

Story

EUREKA

Ideas/Concepts

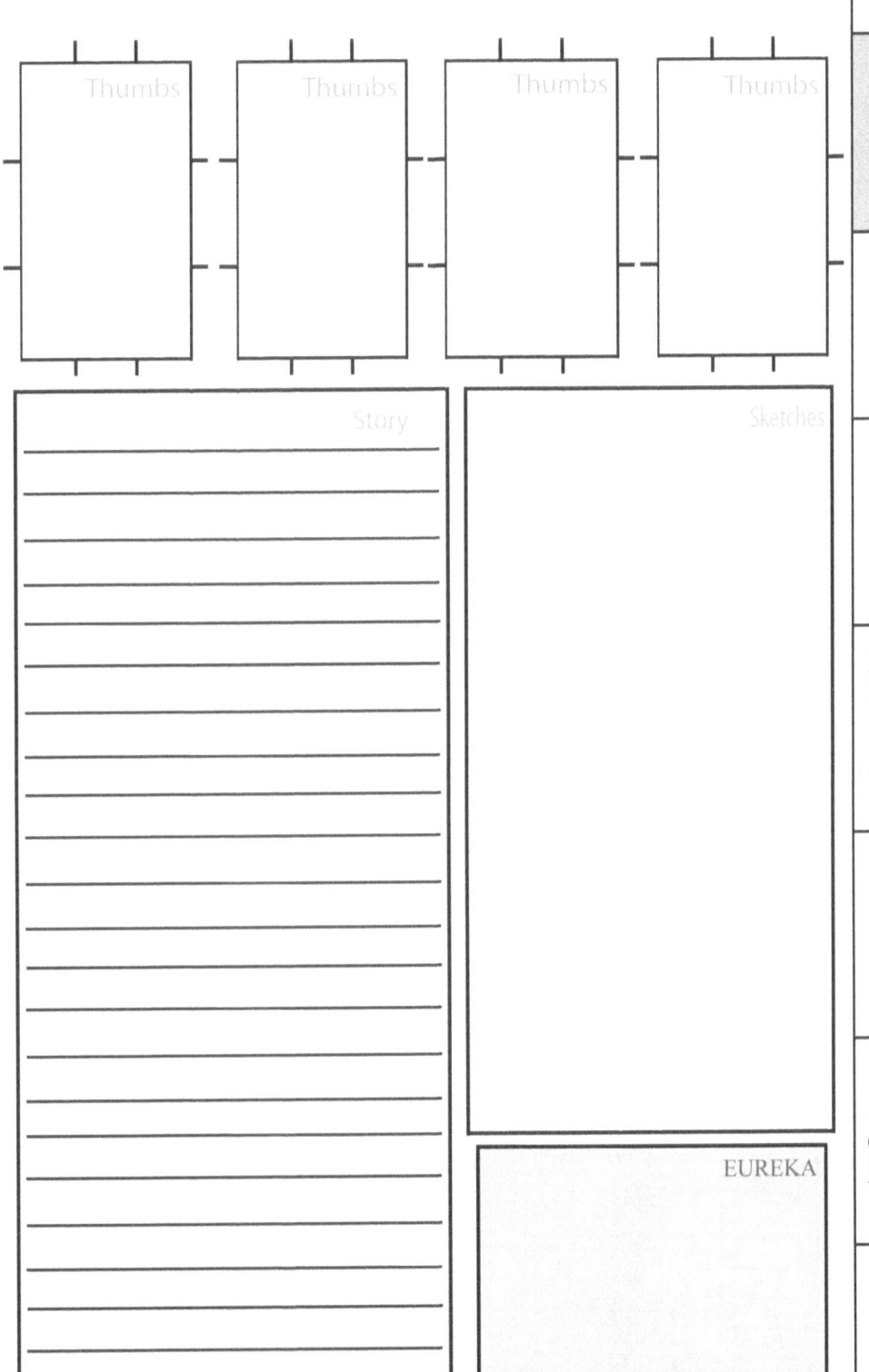

Thumbs   Thumbs   Thumbs   Thumbs

Story

Sketches

EUREKA

PLANNER

IDEAS

STORY

CHARACTER

ENVIRON MENTS

ASSETS

STORY BOARDS

OPEN

PLANNER

IDEAS

STORY

CHARACTER

ENVIRONMENTS

ASSETS

STORY BOARDS

OPEN

Ideas/Concepts

Thumbs

Thumbs

Thumbs

Thumbs

Sketches

Story

EUREKA

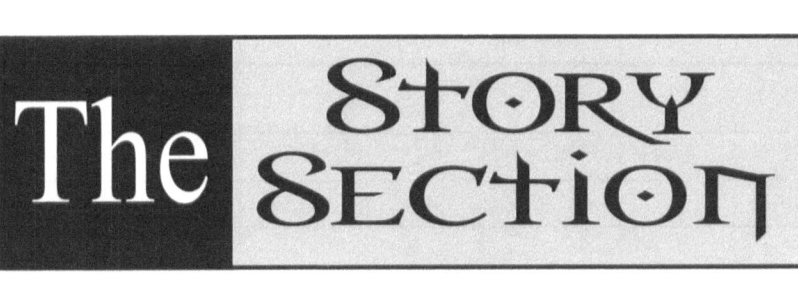
The Story Section

P
L
A
N
N
E
R

I
D
E
A
S

S
T
O
R
Y

C
H
A
R
A
C
T
E
R

E
N
V
I
R
O
N

M
E
N
T
S

A
S
S
E
T
S

S
T
O
R
Y

B
O
A
R
D
S

O
P
E
N

In this section you are to work through you story ideas. Remember this is the most important part of your project.

EUREKA

PLANNER

IDEAS

STORY

CHARACTER

ENVIRONMENTS

ASSETS

STORY BOARDS

OPEN

Story Ideas

Story Notes

EUREKA

Characters

Story Ideas

Characters

EUREKA

PLANNER

IDEAS

STORY

CHARACTER

ENVIRONMENTS

ASSETS

STORY BOARDS

OPEN

PLANNER

IDEAS

STORY

CHARACTER

ENVIRONMENTS

ASSETS

STORYBOARDS

OPEN

Story Summary

Title

Genre

Audience

Medium

Characters

Setting

Conflict

Resolution

EUREKA

Tagline

Main Characters

PLANNER

IDEAS

STORY

CHARACTER

ENVIRONMENTS

ASSETS

STORY BOARDS

OPEN

Protagonist

Name	
Alias	
Age	
Height	
Weight	
Archetype	
Attributes	_____
	_____
	_____
	_____
	_____
Abilities	_____
	_____
	_____
	_____
Story	_____
	_____
	_____
	_____
	_____
	_____
	_____

Antagonist

Name	
Alias	
Age	
Height	
Weight	
Archetype	
Attributes	_____
	_____
	_____
	_____
	_____
Abilities	_____
	_____
	_____
	_____
Story	_____
	_____
	_____
	_____
	_____
	_____
	_____

Conflict
_____
_____
_____
_____

EUREKA

PLANNER

IDEAS

STORY

CHARACTER

ENVIRONMENTS

ASSETS

STORY BOARDS

OPEN

Plot Points

Plot Points

Twist

Story Events

EUREKA

3 Act Stucture

Act One

Setting		Character Introt	
Setting		Character Intro	
Character Intro		Conflict	
Character Introt		Level of Conflict	

Act Two

Rising Action		Rising Action	
Rising Action		Rising Action	
Rising Action		Rising Actiont	
Rising Action		Rising Action	

Act Three

Climax		Falling Action	
Falling Action		Falling Action	
Falling Action		Resolution	
Falling Action		Catharsis	

Story Summary

EUREKA

PLANNER

IDEAS

STORY

CHARACTER

ENVIRONMENTS

ASSETS

STORY BOARDS

OPEN

Plot Diagram

P L A N N E R

I D E A S

S T O R Y

C H A R A C T E R

E N V I R O N

M E N T S

A S S E T S

S T O R Y   B O A R D S

O P E N

Rising Action

Rising Action

Rising Action

Rising Action

Conflicts

Exposition

EUREKA

Extra Story Points

Plot Diagram

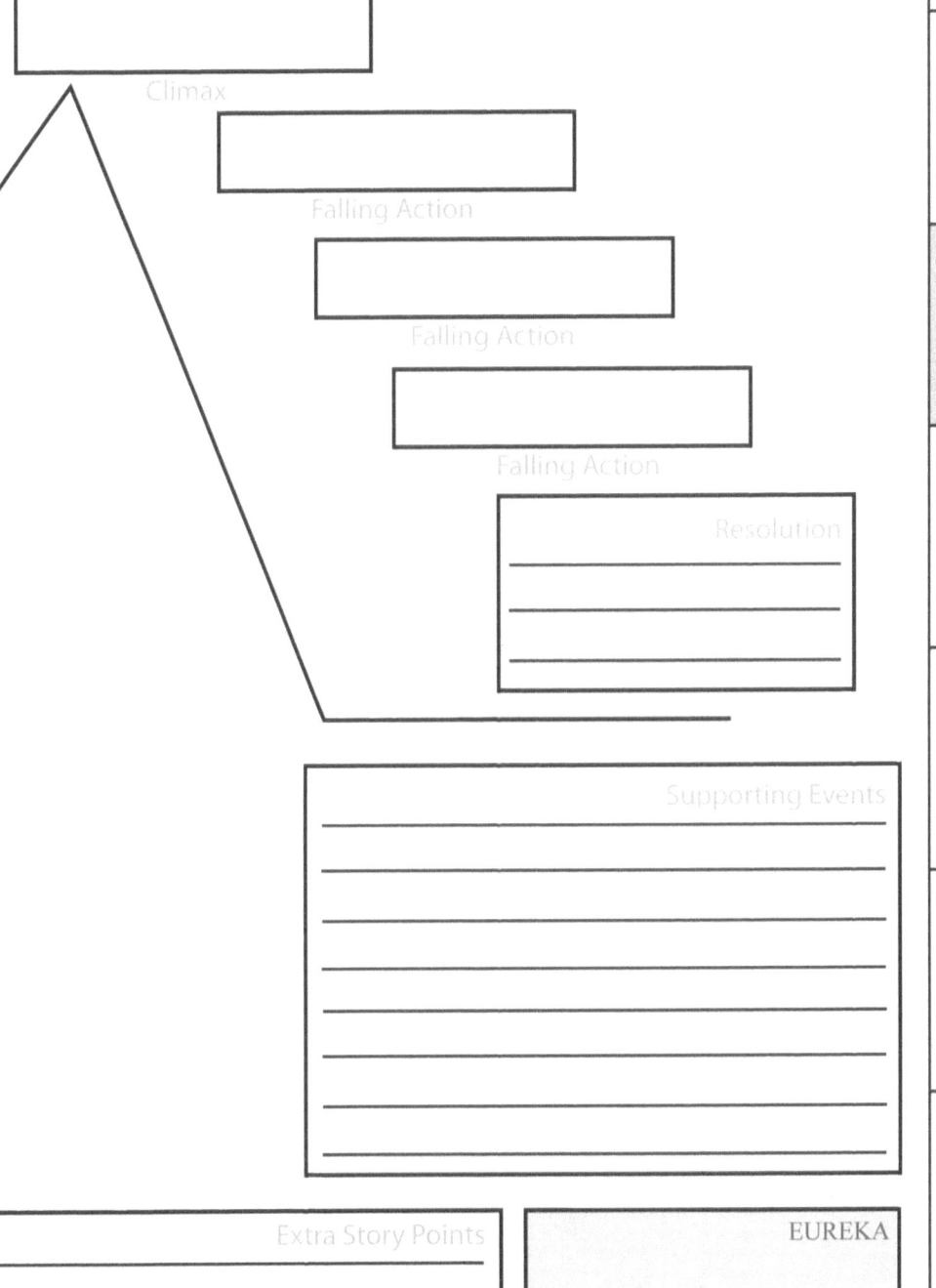

Climax

Falling Action

Falling Action

Falling Action

Resolution

Supporting Events

Extra Story Points

EUREKA

PLANNER

IDEAS

STORY

CHARACTER

ENVIRONMENTS

ASSETS

STORY BOARDS

OPEN

The CHARACTER SECTION

In this section you will be able to flesh out your characters.
Exploring story, turn arounds, facial expressions
and action poses.

EUREKA

Character Sheet

Name	
Alias	
Age	
Height	
Weight	
Archetype	
Attributes	
Abilities	
Timeline	
Primary Weapon	
Secondary Weapon	
Biggest Fear	
Character Flaw	
Weakness	

Strength	OOOOOOOOOO
Dexterity	OOOOOOOOOO
Speed	OOOOOOOOOO
Reflexes	OOOOOOOOOO
Intelligence	OOOOOOOOOO
Wisdom	OOOOOOOOOO
Fighting Skills	OOOOOOOOOO
Endurance	OOOOOOOOOO
Brave	OOOOOOOOOO
Confidence	OOOOOOOOOO
Loyal	OOOOOOOOOO
Creative	OOOOOOOOOO
Studious	OOOOOOOOOO
Lucky	OOOOOOOOOO
Good	OOOOOOOOOO
Evil	OOOOOOOOOO

EUREKA

PLANNER

IDEAS

STORY

CHARACTER

ENVIRONMENTS

ASSETS

STORY BOARDS

OPEN

PLANNER

IDEAS

STORY

CHARACTER

ENVIRONMENTS

ASSETS

STORYBOARDS

OPEN

Character Turns

Body Turn

Head Turn

EUREKA

Color Key

Character Expressions

Static

Happy

Sad

Angry

Confused

Fear

Disgust

Surprised

Pleased

Triumphant

EUREKA

PLANNER

IDEAS

STORY

CHARACTER

ENVIRONMENTS

ASSETS

STORY BOARDS

OPEN

PLANNER

IDEAS

STORY

CHARACTER

ENVIRONMENTS

ASSETS

STORYBOARDS

OPEN

Character Poses

Atacking

Defeated

Suprised

EUREKA

Character Poses

Running

Power Pose

Sitting

EUREKA

PLANNER

IDEAS

STORY

CHARACTER

ENVIRONMENTS

ASSETS

STORYBOARDS

OPEN

Character Sheet

PLANNER

IDEAS

STORY

CHARACTER

ENVIRONMENTS

ASSETS

STORY BOARDS

OPEN

	Attribute
OOOOOOOOOO	Strength
OOOOOOOOOO	Dexterity
OOOOOOOOOO	Speed
OOOOOOOOOO	Reflexes
OOOOOOOOOO	Intellegence
OOOOOOOOOO	Wisdom
OOOOOOOOOO	Fighting Skills
OOOOOOOOOO	Endurance
OOOOOOOOOO	Brave
OOOOOOOOOO	Confidence
OOOOOOOOOO	Loyal
OOOOOOOOOO	Creative
OOOOOOOOOO	Studious
OOOOOOOOOO	Lucky
OOOOOOOOOO	Good
OOOOOOOOOO	Evil

EUREKA

	Name
	Alias
	Age
	Height
	Weight
	Archetype
	Attributes
	Abilities
	Timeline
	Primary Weapon
	Secondary Weapon
	Biggest Fear
	Character Flaw
	Weakness

Character Turns

PLANNER

IDEAS

STORY

CHARACTER

ENVIRONMENTS

ASSETS

STORYBOARDS

OPEN

Head Turn

Color Key

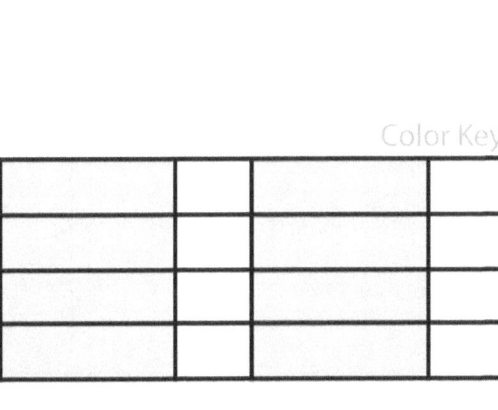

EUREKA

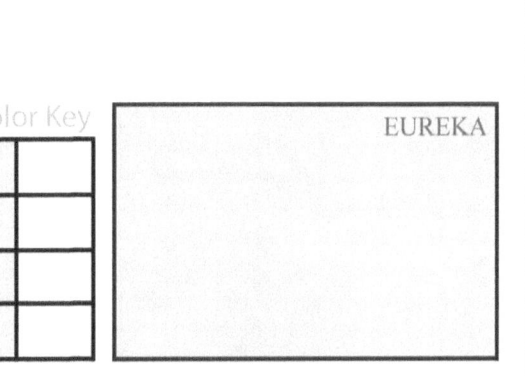

Character Expressions

IDEAS

STORY

CHARACTER

ENVIRONMENTS

ASSETS

STORYBOARDS

OPEN

Static

Happy

Sad

Angry

Confused

Fear

Disgust

Surprised

Pleased

EUREKA

Triumphant

Character Poses

Defeated

Attacking

Surprised

EUREKA

PLANNER

IDEAS

STORY

CHARACTER

ENVIRONMENTS

ASSETS

STORY BOARDS

OPEN

Character Poses

PLANNER

IDEAS

STORY

CHARACTER

ENVIRONMENTS

ASSETS

STORYBOARDS

OPEN

Power Pose

Running

Sitting

EUREKA

Character Sheet

Name	
Alias	
Age	
Height	
Weight	
Archetype	
Attributes	

Abilities

Timeline

Primary Weapon	
Secondary Weapon	
Biggest Fear	
Character Flaw	
Weakness	

Strength	OOOOOOOOOO
Dexterity	OOOOOOOOOO
Speed	OOOOOOOOOO
Reflexes	OOOOOOOOOO
Intelligence	OOOOOOOOOO
Wisdom	OOOOOOOOOO
Fighting Skills	OOOOOOOOOO
Endurance	OOOOOOOOOO
Brave	OOOOOOOOOO
Confidence	OOOOOOOOOO
Loyal	OOOOOOOOOO
Creative	OOOOOOOOOO
Studious	OOOOOOOOOO
Lucky	OOOOOOOOOO
Good	OOOOOOOOOO
Evil	OOOOOOOOOO

EUREKA

PLANNER

IDEAS

STORY

CHARACTER

ENVIRONMENTS

ASSETS

STORY BOARDS

OPEN

PLANNER

IDEAS

STORY

CHARACTER

ENVIRONMENTS

ASSETS

STORY BOARDS

OPEN

Character Turns

Body Turn

Head Turn

EUREKA

Color Key

Character Expressions

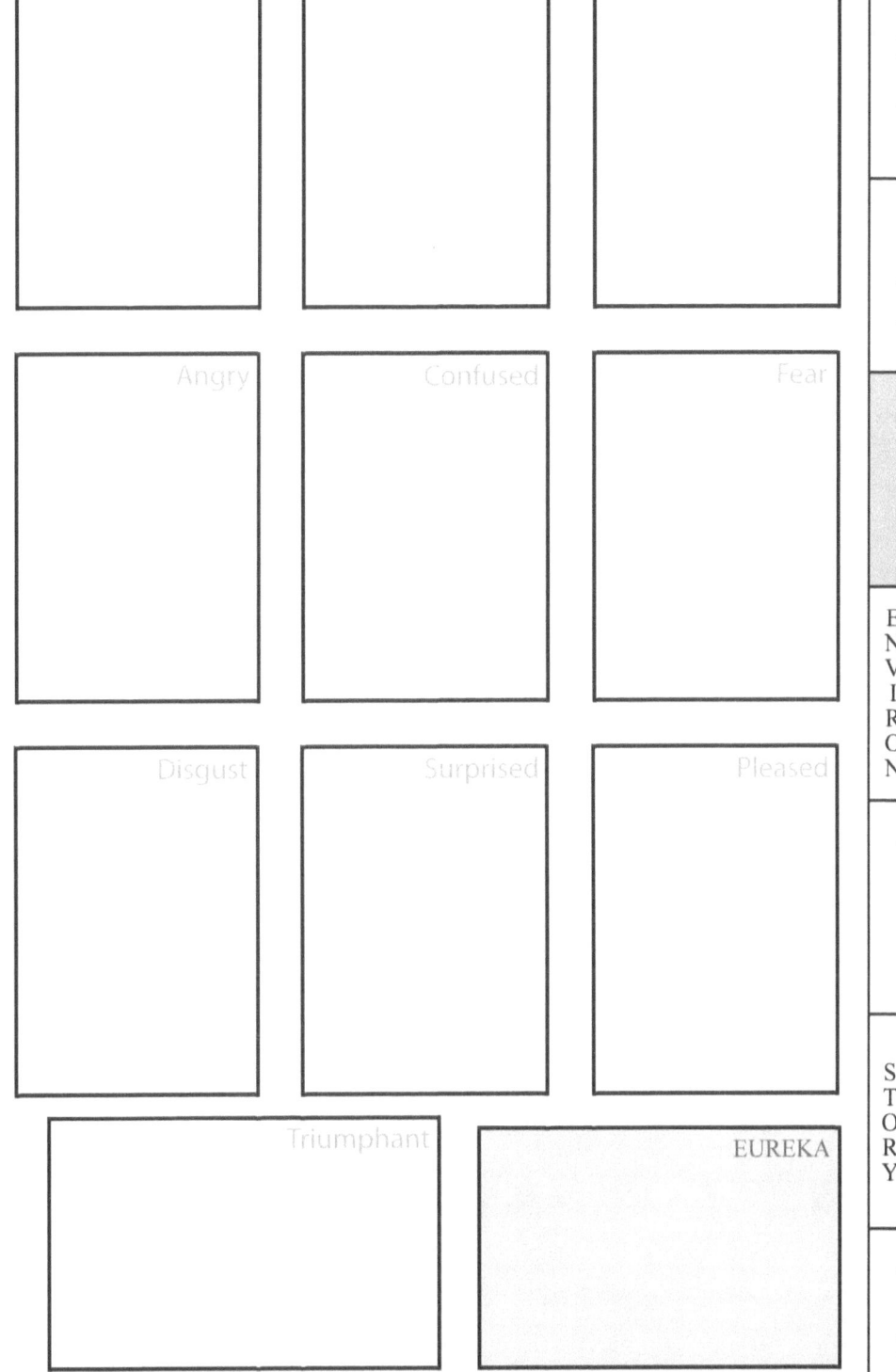

Static

Happy

Sad

Angry

Confused

Fear

Disgust

Surprised

Pleased

Triumphant

EUREKA

PLANNER

IDEAS

STORY

CHARACTER

ENVIRONMENTS

ASSETS

STORY BOARDS

OPEN

PLANNER

IDEAS

STORY

CHARACTER

ENVIRONMENTS

ASSETS

STORYBOARDS

OPEN

Character Poses

Atacking

Defeated

Suprised

EUREKA

Character Poses

Running

Power Pose

Sitting

EUREKA

PLANNER

IDEAS

STORY

CHARACTER

ENVIRONMENTS

ASSETS

STORY BOARDS

OPEN

Character Sheet

PLANNER

IDEAS

STORY

CHARACTER

ENVIRONMENTS

ASSETS

STORY BOARDS

OPEN

OOOOOOOOOO	Strength
OOOOOOOOOO	Dexterity
OOOOOOOOOO	Speed
OOOOOOOOOO	Reflexes
OOOOOOOOOO	Intellegence
OOOOOOOOOO	Wisdom
OOOOOOOOOO	Fighting Skills
OOOOOOOOOO	Endurance
OOOOOOOOOO	Brave
OOOOOOOOOO	Confidence
OOOOOOOOOO	Loyal
OOOOOOOOOO	Creative
OOOOOOOOOO	Studious
OOOOOOOOOO	Lucky
OOOOOOOOOO	Good
OOOOOOOOOO	Evil

EUREKA

	Name
	Alias
	Age
	Height
	Weight
	Archetype
	Attributes
	Abilities
	Timeline
	Primary Weapon
	Secondary Weapon
	Biggest Fear
	Character Flaw
	Weakness

Character Turns

PLANNER

IDEAS

STORY

CHARACTER

ENVIRONMENTS

ASSETS

STORYBOARDS

OPEN

Body Turn

Head Turn

Color Key

EUREKA

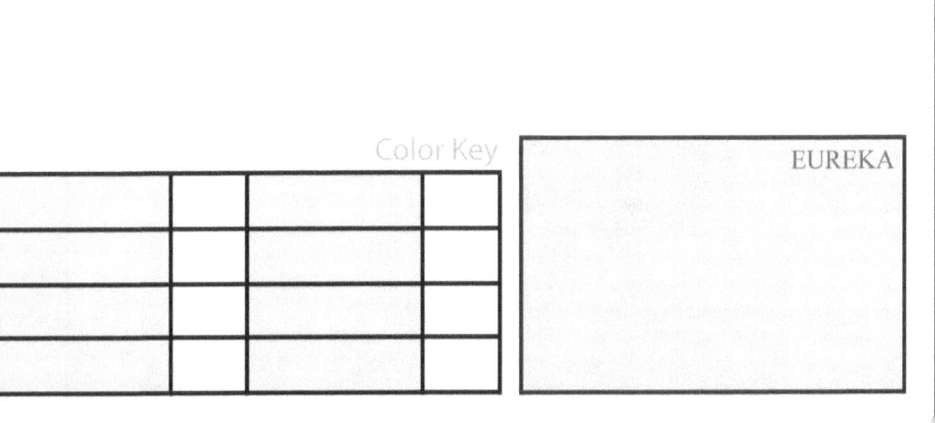

Character Expressions

Static

Happy

Sad

Angry

Confused

Fear

Disgust

Surprised

Pleased

EUREKA

Triumphant

Character Poses

Defeated

Attacking

Surprised

EUREKA

PLANNER

IDEAS

STORY

CHARACTER

ENVIRONMENTS

ASSETS

STORYBOARDS

OPEN

Character Poses

PLANNER

IDEAS

STORY

CHARACTER

ENVIRONMENTS

ASSETS

STORYBOARDS

OPEN

Power Pose

Running

Sitting

EUREKA

The Environment Section

In this section you should try and cement a concept for some of your environmental settings where your story will take place.

PLANNER

IDEAS

STORY

CHARACTER

ENVIRONMENTS

ASSETS

STORY BOARDS

OPEN

EUREKA

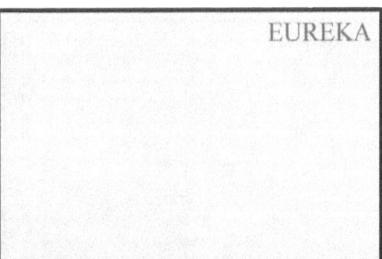

PLANNER

IDEAS

STORY

CHARACTER

ENVIRON MENTS

ASSETS

STORY BOARDS

OPEN

Reference

Reference Images

Notes

EUREKA

Reference

Notes

EUREKA

PLANNER

IDEAS

STORY

CHARACTER

ENVIRONMENTS

ASSETS

STORY BOARDS

OPEN

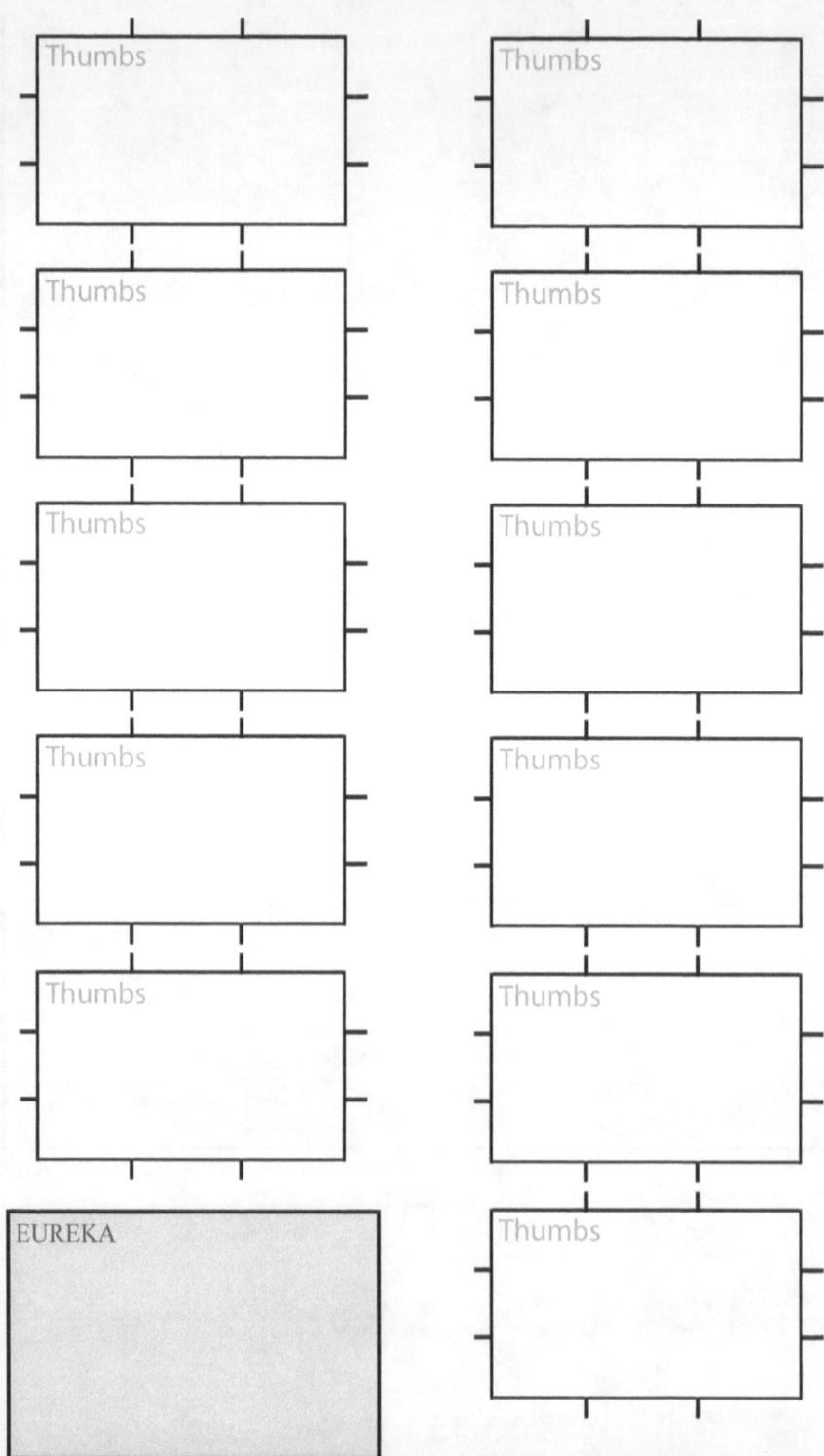

Environment Ideas

PLANNER

IDEAS

STORY

CHARACTER

ENVIRONMENTS

ASSETS

STORY BOARDS

OPEN

Thumbs

Thumbs

Thumbs

Thumbs

Thumbs

Thumbs

Thumbs

Thumbs

Thumbs

EUREKA

Thumbs

Environment Render

Render

Render

Color Key

EUREKA

PLANNER

IDEAS

STORY

CHARACTER

ENVIRONMENTS

ASSETS

STORY BOARDS

OPEN

PLANNER

IDEAS

STORY

CHARACTER

ENVIRONMENTS

ASSETS

STORY BOARDS

OPEN

Environment Ideas

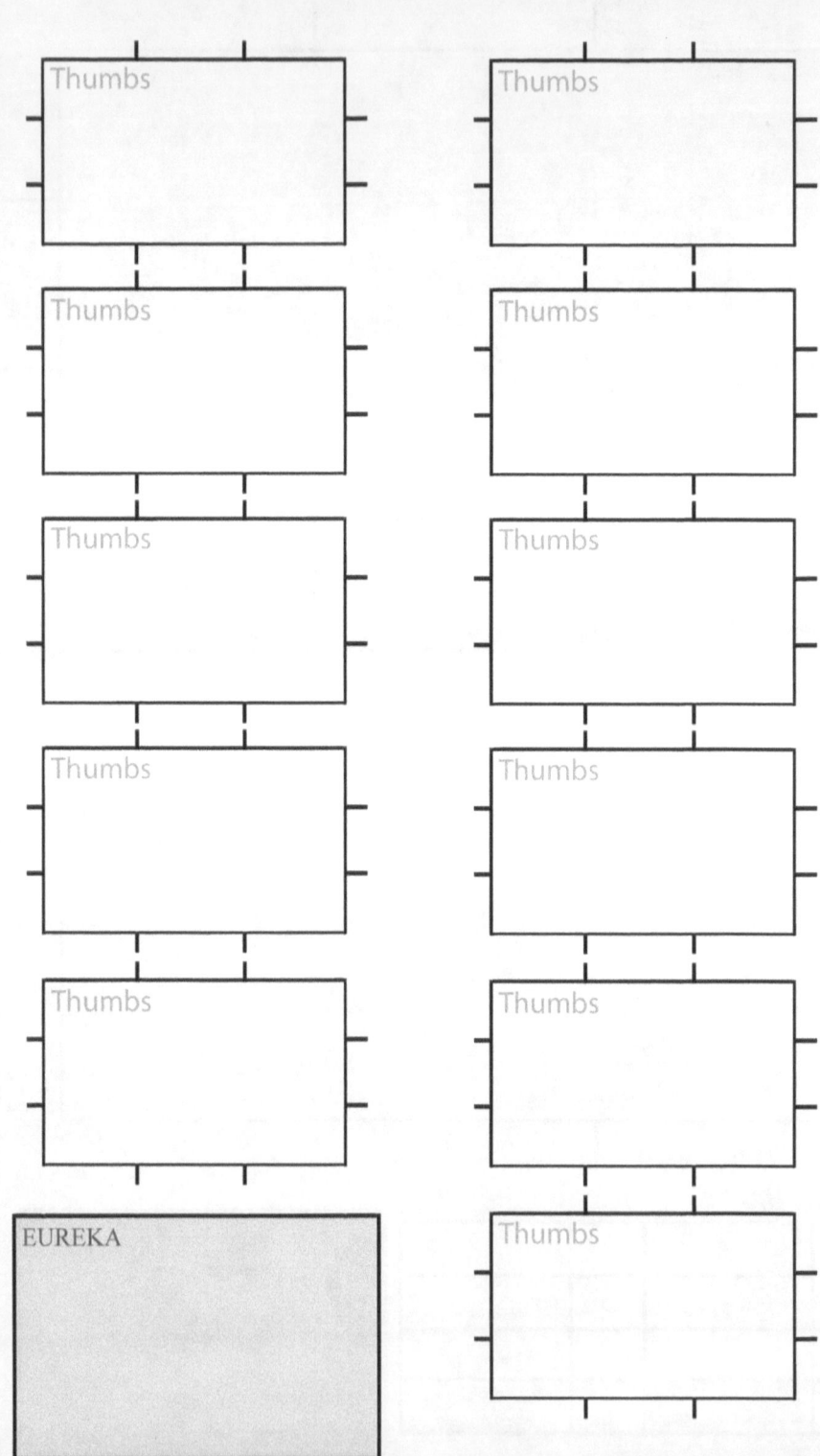

Environment Render

Render

Render

Color Key

EUREKA

PLANNER

IDEAS

STORY

CHARACTER

ENVIRONMENTS

ASSETS

STORY BOARDS

OPEN

Environment Ideas

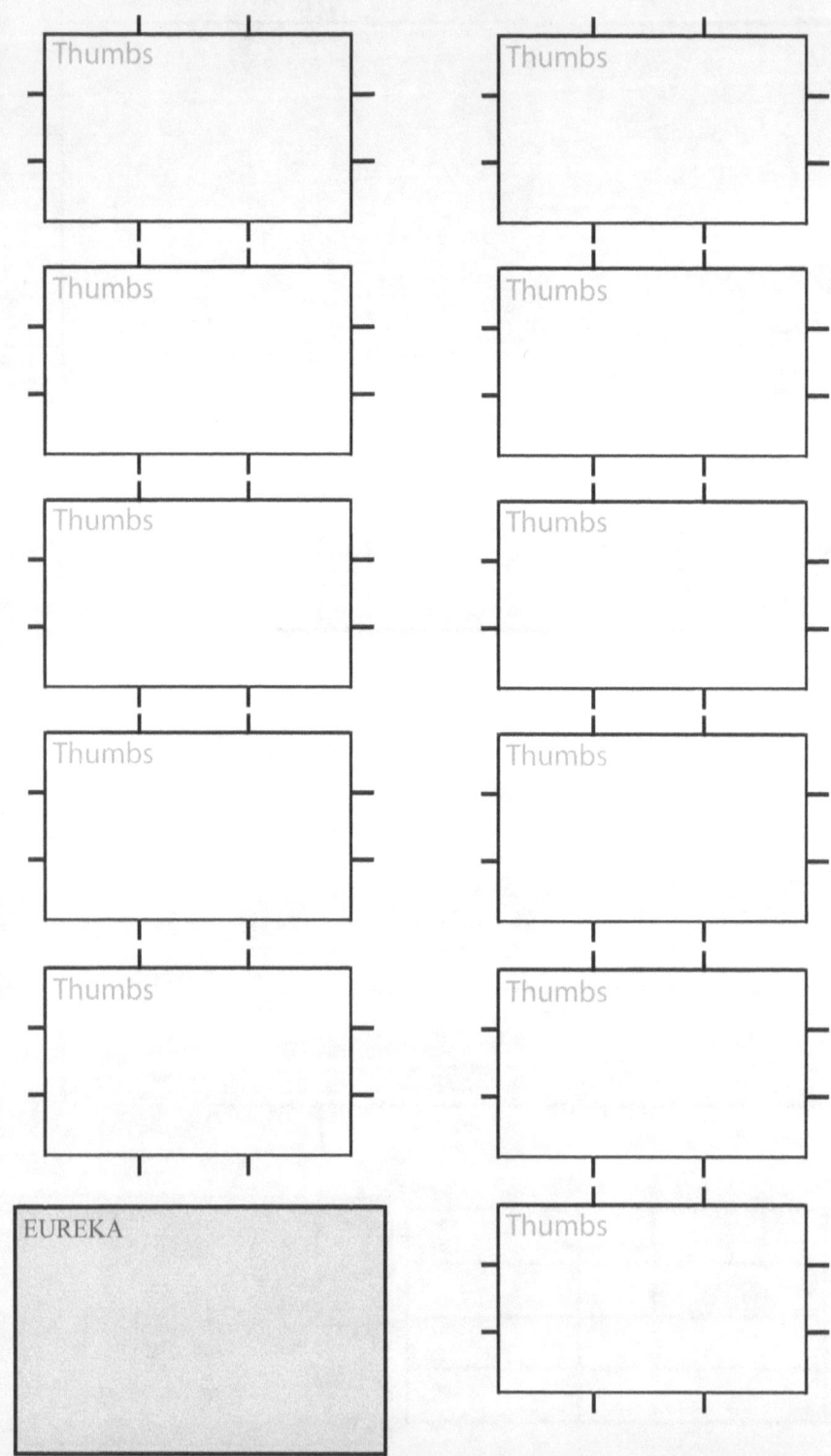

PLANNER

IDEAS

STORY

CHARACTER

ENVIRONMENTS

ASSETS

STORY BOARDS

OPEN

Thumbs

Thumbs

Thumbs

Thumbs

Thumbs

Thumbs

Thumbs

Thumbs

Thumbs

EUREKA

Thumbs

Environment Render

Render

Render

Color Key

EUREKA

PLANNER

IDEAS

STORY

CHARACTER

ENVIRONMENTS

ASSETS

STORY BOARDS

OPEN

PLANNER

IDEAS

STORY

CHARACTER

ENVIRONMENTS

ASSETS

STORYBOARDS

OPEN

Environment Ideas

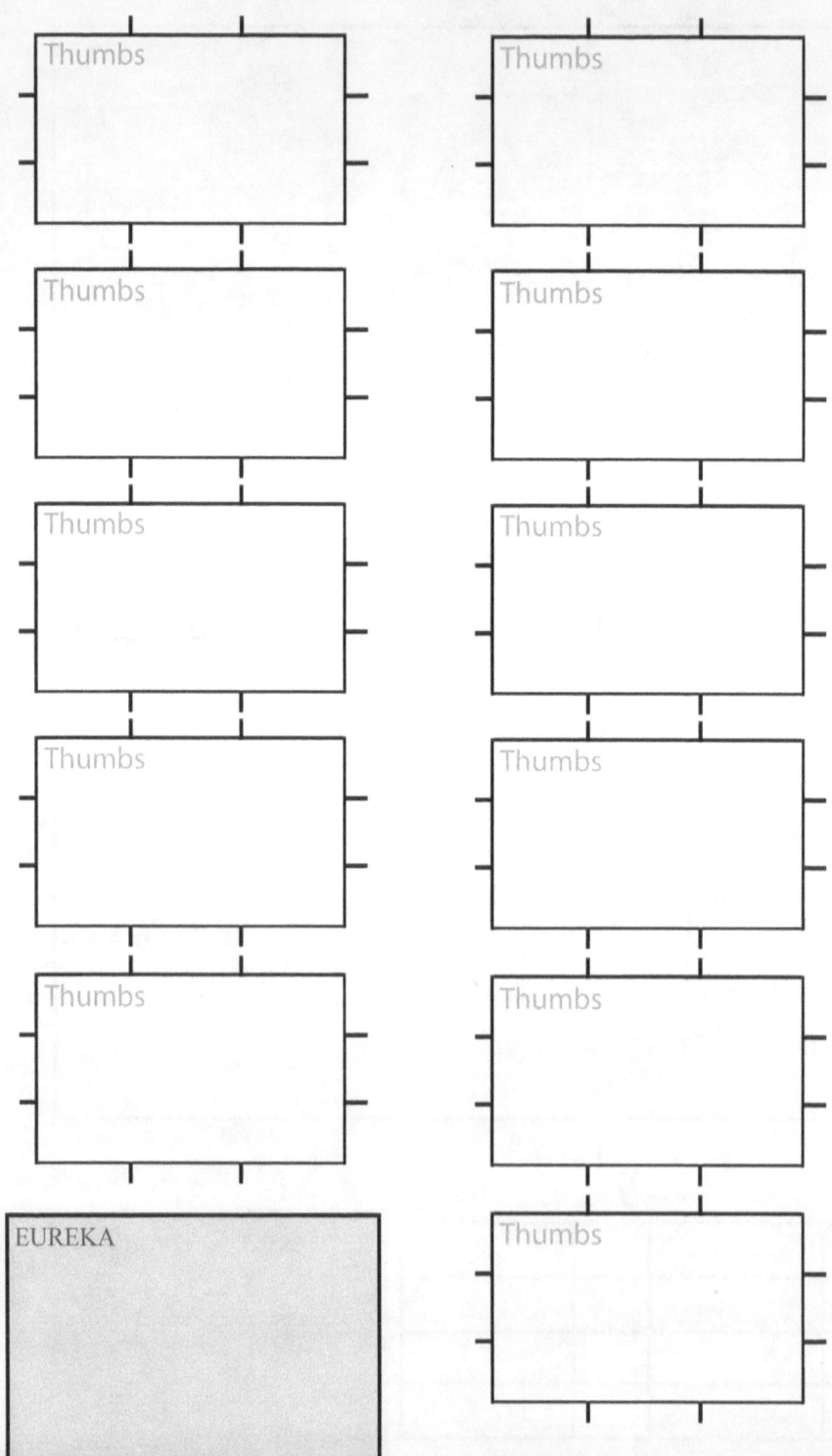

Thumbs

Thumbs

Thumbs

Thumbs

Thumbs

Thumbs

Thumbs

Thumbs

Thumbs

Thumbs

EUREKA

Thumbs

Environment Render

Render

Render

Color Key

EUREKA

PLANNER

IDEAS

STORY

CHARACTER

ENVIRONMENTS

ASSETS

STORY BOARDS

OPEN

PLANNER

IDEAS

STORY

CHARACTER

ENVIRON MENTS

ASSETS

STORY BOARDS

OPEN

Environment Ideas

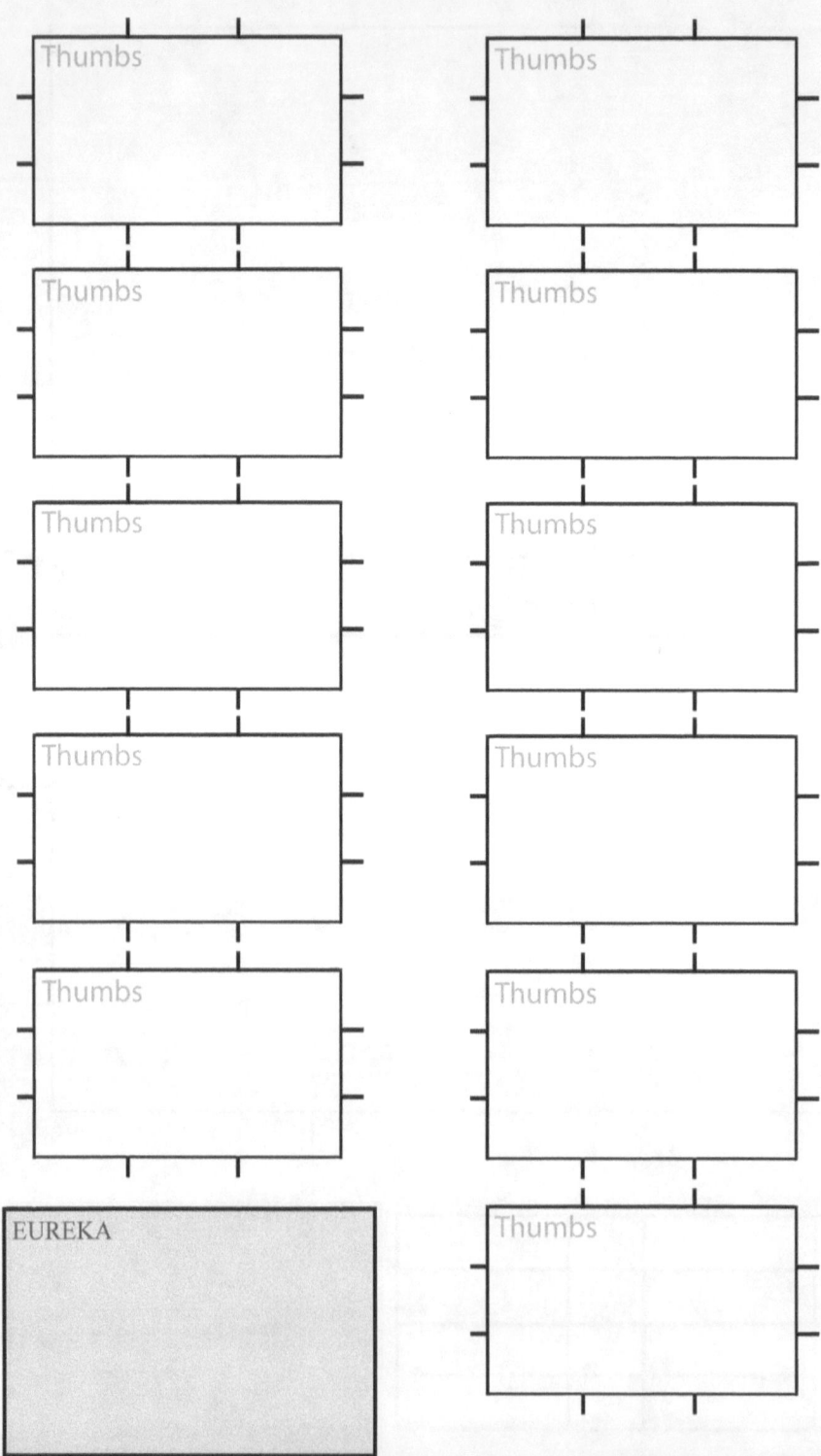

Thumbs

Thumbs

Thumbs

Thumbs

Thumbs

Thumbs

Thumbs

Thumbs

Thumbs

EUREKA

Thumbs

Environment Render

Render

Render

Color Key

EUREKA

PLANNER

IDEAS

STORY

CHARACTER

ENVIRONMENTS

ASSETS

STORY BOARDS

OPEN

The ASSET SECTION

In this section you should think of all the things that are extras, but are still very important to your environment, characters and story.

EUREKA

Assets

PLANNER

IDEAS

STORY

CHARACTER

ENVIRONMENTS

ASSETS

STORYBOARDS

OPEN

Fashion/Weapons/Armor

Important Items

Current Technology

Symbols

EUREKA

PLANNER

IDEAS

STORY

CHARACTER

ENVIRONMENTS

ASSETS

STORY BOARDS

OPEN

Assets

Fashion/Weapons/Armor

Important Items

Current Technology

EUREKA

Symbols

Assets

Fashion/Weapons/Armor

Important Items

Current Technology

Symbols

EUREKA

PLANNER

IDEAS

STORY

CHARACTER

ENVIRONMENTS

ASSETS

STORY BOARDS

OPEN

PLANNER

IDEAS

STORY

CHARACTER

ENVIRONMENTS

ASSETS

STORY BOARDS

OPEN

Assets

Fashion/Weapons/Armor

Important Items

Current Technology

EUREKA

Symbols

Assets

Fashion/Weapons/Armor

Important Items

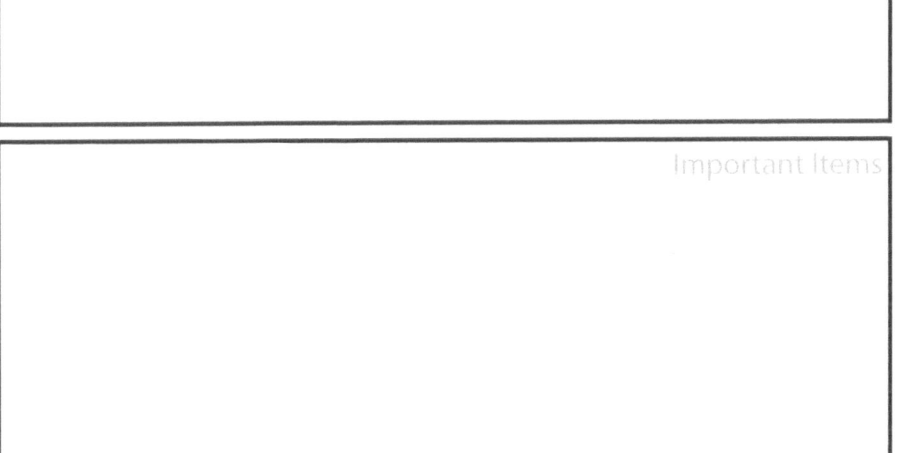

Current Technology

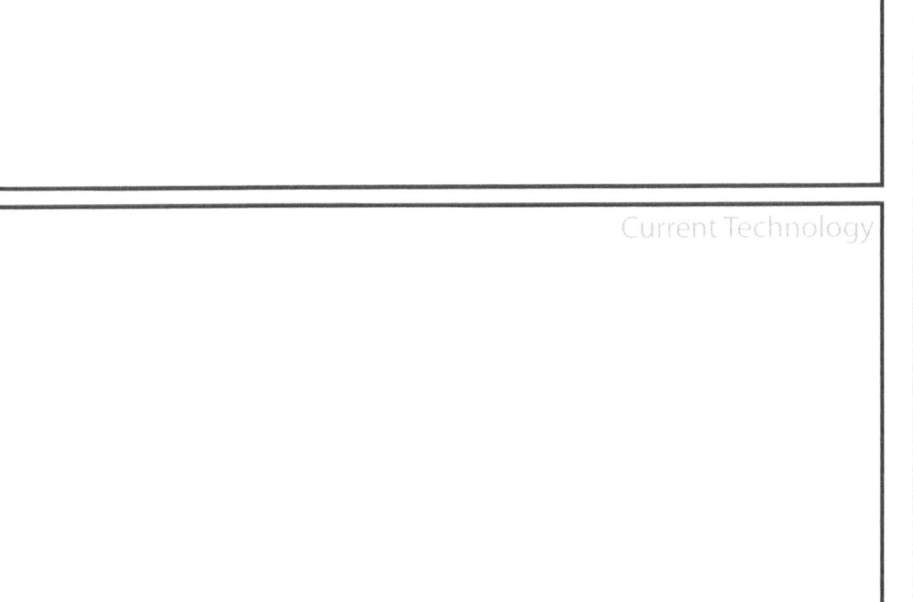

Symbols

EUREKA

PLANNER

IDEAS

STORY

CHARACTER

ENVIRONMENTS

ASSETS

STORY BOARDS

OPEN

PLANNER

IDEAS

STORY

CHARACTER

ENVIRONMENTS

ASSETS

STORYBOARDS

OPEN

Assets

Fashion/Weapons/Armor

Important Items

Current Technology

EUREKA

Symbols

Assets

Fashion/Weapons/Armor

Important Items

Current Technology

Symbols

EUREKA

PLANNER

IDEAS

STORY

CHARACTER

ENVIRONMENTS

ASSETS

STORY BOARDS

OPEN

PLANNER

IDEAS

STORY

CHARACTER

ENVIRONMENTS

ASSETS

STORYBOARDS

OPEN

Assets

Fashion/Weapons/Armor

Important Items

Current Technology

EUREKA

Symbols

Assets

Fashion/Weapons/Armor

Important Items

Current Technology

Symbols

EUREKA

PLANNER

IDEAS

STORY

CHARACTER

ENVIRONMENTS

ASSETS

STORYBOARDS

OPEN

PLANNER

IDEAS

STORY

CHARACTER

ENVIRONMENTS

ASSETS

STORY BOARDS

OPEN

Assets

Fashion/Weapons/Armor

Important Items

Current Technology

EUREKA

Symbols

The STORYBOARD SECTION

Story is a very important part of a pitch and in this section you will be able to visually depict a specific scene from your story sequentially.

EUREKA

PLANNER

IDEAS

STORY

CHARACTER

ENVIRONMENTS

ASSETS

STORY BOARDS

OPEN

Scene Script

Scene Description

Story Beats

Shots

Dialog

EUREKA

Storyboards

PLANNER

IDEAS

STORY

CHARACTER

ENVIRONMENTS

ASSETS

STORY BOARDS

OPEN

Full

Wide

Shot		Action	
Duration		Effects	
Dialog			

Full

Wide

Shot		Action	
Duration		Effects	
Dialog			

Full

Wide

Shot		Action	
Duration		Effects	
Dialog			

Full

Wide

Shot		Action	
Duration		Effects	
Dialog			

Full

Wide

Shot		Action	
Duration		Effects	
Dialog			

Full

Wide

Shot		Action	
Duration		Effects	
Dialog			

EUREKA

PLANNER

IDEAS

STORY

CHARACTER

ENVIRONMENTS

ASSETS

STORYBOARDS

OPEN

Storyboards

Full

Wide

Shot		Action	
Duration		Effects	
Dialog			

Full

Wide

Shot		Action	
Duration		Effects	
Dialog			

Full

Wide

Shot		Action	
Duration		Effects	
Dialog			

EUREKA

Full

Wide

Shot		Action	
Duration		Effects	
Dialog			

Full

Wide

Shot		Action	
Duration		Effects	
Dialog			

Full

Wide

Shot		Action	
Duration		Effects	
Dialog			

Full

Wide

Storyboards

PLANNER

IDEAS

STORY

CHARACTER

ENVIRONMENTS

ASSETS

STORYBOARDS

OPEN

Full

Wide

Shot		Action	
Duration		Effects	
Dialog			

Full

Wide

Shot		Action	
Duration		Effects	
Dialog			

Full

Wide

Shot		Action	
Duration		Effects	
Dialog			

Full

Wide

Shot		Action	
Duration		Effects	
Dialog			

Full

Wide

Shot		Action	
Duration		Effects	
Dialog			

Full

Wide

Shot		Action	
Duration		Effects	
Dialog			

EUREKA

PLANNER

IDEAS

STORY

CHARACTER

ENVIRONMENTS

ASSETS

STORYBOARDS

OPEN

Storyboards

Full

Wide

Shot		Action	
Duration		Effects	
Dialog			

Full

Wide

Shot		Action	
Duration		Effects	
Dialog			

Full

Wide

Shot		Action	
Duration		Effects	
Dialog			

Full

Wide

Shot		Action	
Duration		Effects	
Dialog			

Full

Wide

Shot		Action	
Duration		Effects	
Dialog			

Full

Wide

Shot		Action	
Duration		Effects	
Dialog			

EUREKA

Full

Wide

Storyboards

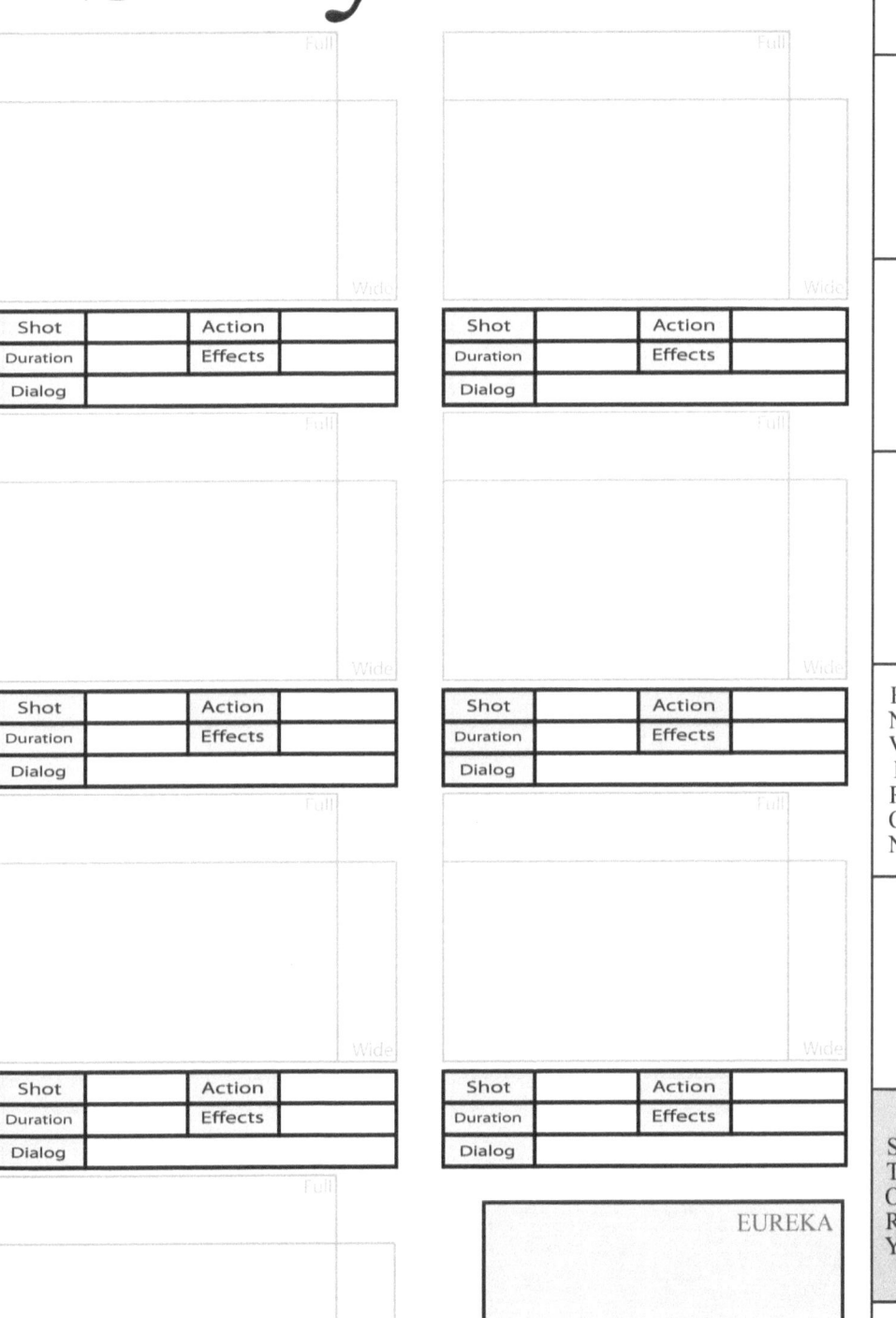

Shot		Action	
Duration		Effects	
Dialog			

Shot		Action	
Duration		Effects	
Dialog			

Shot		Action	
Duration		Effects	
Dialog			

Shot		Action	
Duration		Effects	
Dialog			

Shot		Action	
Duration		Effects	
Dialog			

Shot		Action	
Duration		Effects	
Dialog			

EUREKA

PLANNER

IDEAS

STORY

CHARACTER

ENVIRONMENTS

ASSETS

STORYBOARDS

OPEN

PLANNER

IDEAS

STORY

CHARACTER

ENVIRONMENTS

ASSETS

STORYBOARDS

OPEN

Storyboards

Full

Wide

Shot		Action	
Duration		Effects	
Dialog			

Full

Wide

Shot		Action	
Duration		Effects	
Dialog			

Full

Wide

Shot		Action	
Duration		Effects	
Dialog			

Full

Wide

Shot		Action	
Duration		Effects	
Dialog			

Full

Wide

Shot		Action	
Duration		Effects	
Dialog			

Full

Wide

Shot		Action	
Duration		Effects	
Dialog			

EUREKA

Full

Wide

Storyboards

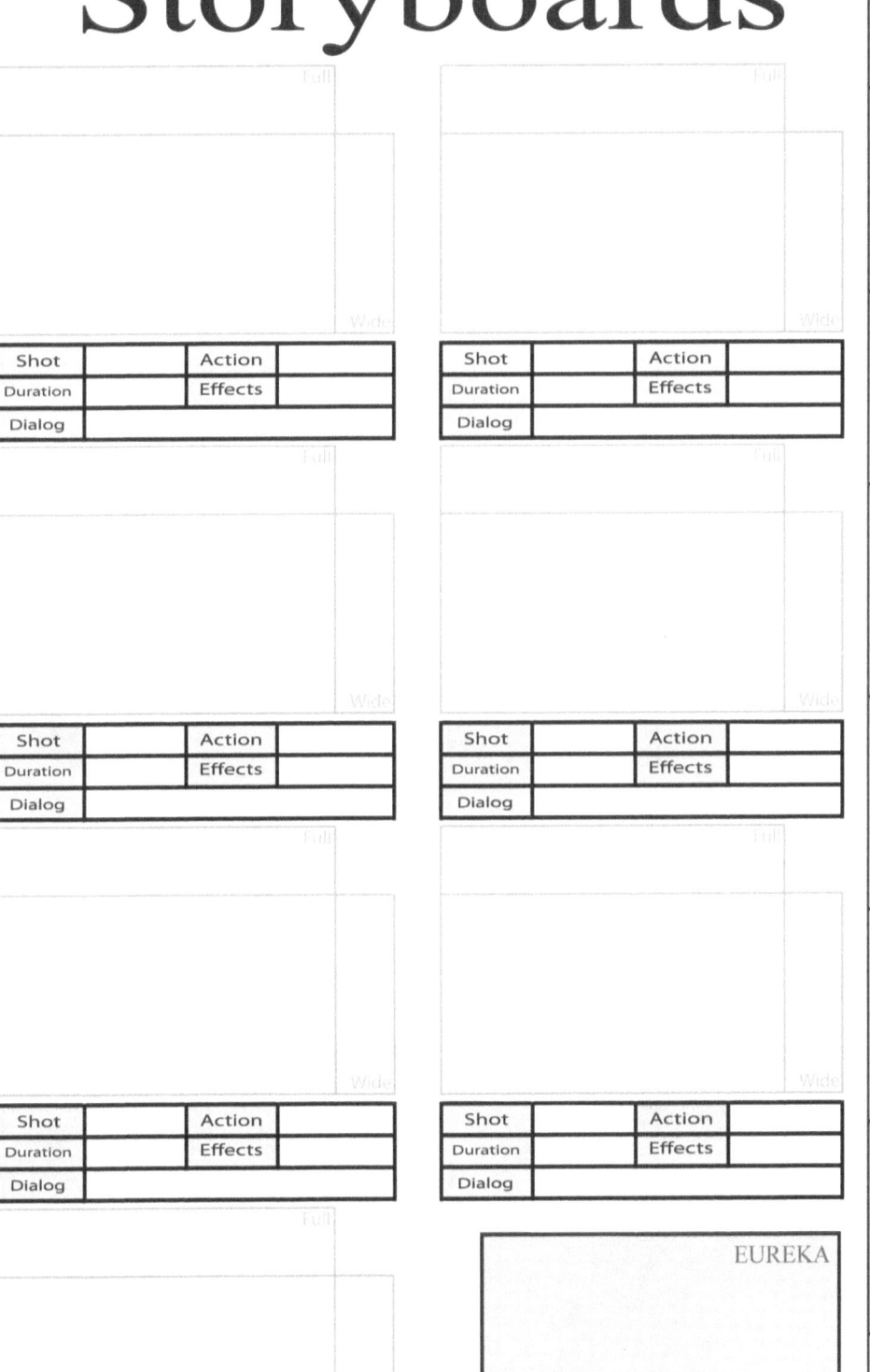

Shot		Action	
Duration		Effects	
Dialog			

Shot		Action	
Duration		Effects	
Dialog			

Shot		Action	
Duration		Effects	
Dialog			

Shot		Action	
Duration		Effects	
Dialog			

Shot		Action	
Duration		Effects	
Dialog			

Shot		Action	
Duration		Effects	
Dialog			

EUREKA

PLANNER

IDEAS

STORY

CHARACTER

ENVIRONMENTS

ASSETS

STORYBOARDS

OPEN

PLANNER

IDEAS

STORY

CHARACTER

ENVIRON MENTS

ASSETS

STORY BOARDS

OPEN

Storyboards

Full

Wide

Shot		Action	
Duration		Effects	
Dialog			

Full

Wide

Shot		Action	
Duration		Effects	
Dialog			

Full

Wide

Shot		Action	
Duration		Effects	
Dialog			

EUREKA

Full

Wide

Shot		Action	
Duration		Effects	
Dialog			

Full

Wide

Shot		Action	
Duration		Effects	
Dialog			

Full

Wide

Shot		Action	
Duration		Effects	
Dialog			

Full

Wide

Storyboards

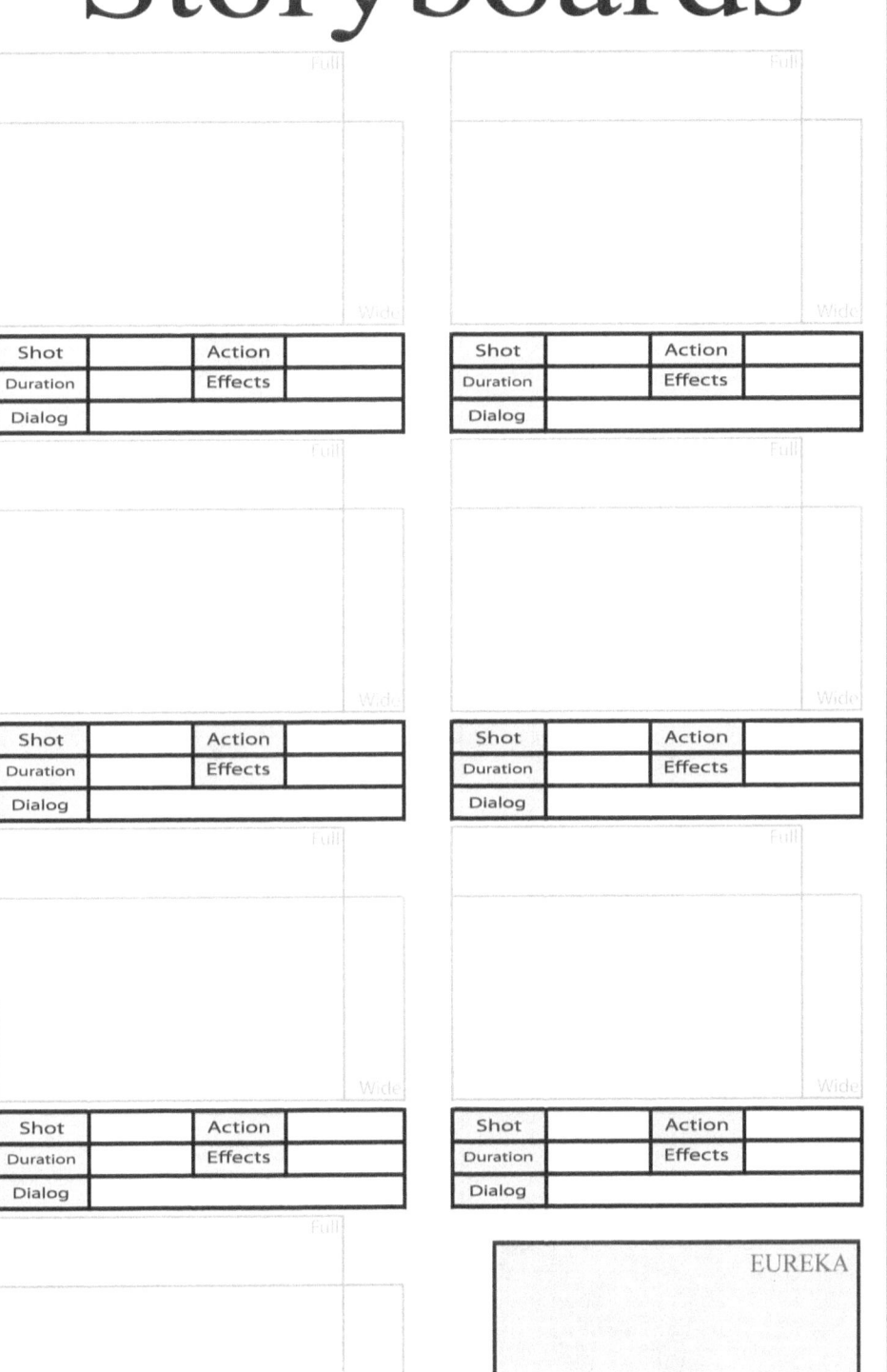

Shot		Action	
Duration		Effects	
Dialog			

Shot		Action	
Duration		Effects	
Dialog			

Shot		Action	
Duration		Effects	
Dialog			

Shot		Action	
Duration		Effects	
Dialog			

Shot		Action	
Duration		Effects	
Dialog			

Shot		Action	
Duration		Effects	
Dialog			

EUREKA

PLANNER

IDEAS

STORY

CHARACTER

ENVIRONMENTS

ASSETS

STORY BOARDS

OPEN

PLANNER

IDEAS

STORY

CHARACTER

ENVIRONMENTS

ASSETS

STORY BOARDS

OPEN

Storyboards

Full

Wide

Shot		Action	
Duration		Effects	
Dialog			

Full

Wide

Shot		Action	
Duration		Effects	
Dialog			

Full

Wide

Shot		Action	
Duration		Effects	
Dialog			

Full

Wide

Shot		Action	
Duration		Effects	
Dialog			

Full

Wide

Shot		Action	
Duration		Effects	
Dialog			

Full

Wide

Shot		Action	
Duration		Effects	
Dialog			

EUREKA

Full

Wide

The FREE SECTION

In this section you have the ability to expand on anything for your project that you might not have had the space for in the rest of the book.

EUREKA

PLANNER

IDEAS

STORY

CHARACTER

ENVIRONMENTS

ASSETS

STORY BOARDS

OPEN

PLANNER

IDEAS

STORY

CHARACTER

ENVIRONMENTS

ASSETS

STORY BOARDS

OPEN

Free For All

Free For All

PLANNER

IDEAS

STORY

CHARACTER

ENVIRONMENTS

ASSETS

STORYBOARDS

OPEN

PLANNER

IDEAS

STORY

CHARACTER

ENVIRON MENTS

ASSETS

STORY BOARDS

OPEN

Free For All

Free For All

PLANNER

IDEAS

STORY

CHARACTER

ENVIRONMENTS

ASSETS

STORY BOARDS

OPEN

PLANNER

IDEAS

STORY

CHARACTER

ENVIRON MENTS

ASSETS

STORY BOARDS

OPEN

Free For All

Free For All

PLANNER

IDEAS

STORY

CHARACTER

ENVIRONMENTS

ASSETS

STORYBOARDS

OPEN

Free For All

PLANNER

IDEAS

STORY

CHARACTER

ENVIRONMENTS

ASSETS

STORY BOARDS

OPEN

Free For All

PLANNER

IDEAS

STORY

CHARACTER

ENVIRONMENTS

ASSETS

STORY BOARDS

OPEN

PLANNER

IDEAS

STORY

CHARACTER

ENVIRONMENTS

ASSETS

STORYBOARDS

OPEN

Free For All

Free For All

PLANNER

IDEAS

STORY

CHARACTER

ENVIRONMENTS

ASSETS

STORYBOARDS

OPEN

PLANNER

IDEAS

STORY

CHARACTER

ENVIRONMENTS

ASSETS

STORY BOARDS

OPEN

Free For All

Free For All

PLANNER

IDEAS

STORY

CHARACTER

ENVIRONMENTS

ASSETS

STORY BOARDS

OPEN

PLANNER

IDEAS

STORY

CHARACTER

ENVIRON MENTS

ASSETS

STORY BOARDS

OPEN

Free For All

Free For All

PLANNER

IDEAS

STORY

CHARACTER

ENVIRONMENTS

ASSETS

STORY BOARDS

OPEN

PLANNER

IDEAS

STORY

CHARACTER

ENVIRONMENTS

ASSETS

STORY BOARDS

OPEN

Free For All

Free For All

PLANNER

IDEAS

STORY

CHARACTER

ENVIRONMENTS

ASSETS

STORYBOARDS

OPEN

Free For All

PLANNER

IDEAS

STORY

CHARACTER

ENVIRONMENTS

ASSETS

STORY BOARDS

OPEN

Free For All

P
L
A
N
N
E
R

I
D
E
A
S

S
T
O
R
Y

C
H
A
R
A
C
T
E
R

E
N
V
I
R
O
N

M
E
N
T
S

A
S
S
E
T
S

S
T
O
R
Y
B
O
A
R
D
S

O
P
E
N

PLANNER

IDEAS

STORY

CHARACTER

ENVIRON MENTS

ASSETS

STORY BOARDS

OPEN

Free For All

Free For All

PLANNER

IDEAS

STORY

CHARACTER

ENVIRONMENTS

ASSETS

STORYBOARDS

OPEN

PLANNER

IDEAS

STORY

CHARACTER

ENVIRON MENTS

ASSETS

STORY BOARDS

OPEN

Free For All

Free For All

PLANNER

IDEAS

STORY

CHARACTER

ENVIRONMENTS

ASSETS

STORY BOARDS

OPEN

PLANNER

IDEAS

STORY

CHARACTER

ENVIRON MENTS

ASSETS

STORY BOARDS

OPEN

Free For All

Free For All

PLANNER

IDEAS

STORY

CHARACTER

ENVIRONMENTS

ASSETS

STORY BOARDS

OPEN

PLANNER

IDEAS

STORY

CHARACTER

ENVIRON MENTS

ASSETS

STORY BOARDS

OPEN

Free For All

Free For All

PLANNER

IDEAS

STORY

CHARACTER

ENVIRONMENTS

ASSETS

STORYBOARDS

OPEN

PLANNER

IDEAS

STORY

CHARACTER

ENVIRONMENTS

ASSETS

STORY BOARDS

OPEN

Free For All

Free For All

PLANNER

IDEAS

STORY

CHARACTER

ENVIRONMENTS

ASSETS

STORY BOARDS

OPEN

PLANNER

IDEAS

STORY

CHARACTER

ENVIRONMENTS

ASSETS

STORY BOARDS

OPEN

Free For All

Free For All

PLANNER

IDEAS

STORY

CHARACTER

ENVIRONMENTS

ASSETS

STORYBOARDS

OPEN

PLANNER

IDEAS

STORY

CHARACTER

ENVIRON MENTS

ASSETS

STORY BOARDS

OPEN

Free For All

Free For All

PLANNER

IDEAS

STORY

CHARACTER

ENVIRONMENTS

ASSETS

STORY BOARDS

OPEN

PLANNER

IDEAS

STORY

CHARACTER

ENVIRONMENTS

ASSETS

STORY BOARDS

OPEN

Free For All

Free For All

PLANNER

IDEAS

STORY

CHARACTER

ENVIRONMENTS

ASSETS

STORYBOARDS

OPEN

PLANNER

IDEAS

STORY

CHARACTER

ENVIRON MENTS

ASSETS

STORY BOARDS

OPEN

Free For All

Free For All

PLANNER

IDEAS

STORY

CHARACTER

ENVIRONMENTS

ASSETS

STORYBOARDS

OPEN

Free For All

PLANNER

IDEAS

STORY

CHARACTER

ENVIRONMENTS

ASSETS

STORY BOARDS

OPEN

Free For All

PLANNER

IDEAS

STORY

CHARACTER

ENVIRONMENTS

ASSETS

STORYBOARDS

OPEN

PLANNER

IDEAS

STORY

CHARACTER

ENVIRON MENTS

ASSETS

STORY BOARDS

OPEN

Free For All